Modern Irish Drama

Irish Studies

Modern Irish Drama

W. B. Yeats to Marina Carr

SECOND EDITION

Sanford Sternlicht

SYRACUSE UNIVERSITY PRESS

Copyright © 2010 by Syracuse University Press
Syracuse, New York 13244-5290

All Rights Reserved

First edition, *A Reader's Guide to Modern Irish Drama*, 1998
Second edition 2010

10 11 12 13 14 15   6 5 4 3 2 1

∞ The paper used in this publication meets the minimum requirements
of the American National Standard for Information Sciences—Permanence
of Paper for Printed Library Materials, ANSI Z39.48-1992.

For a listing of books published and distributed by Syracuse University Press,
visit our Web site at SyracuseUniversityPress.syr.edu.

ISBN: 978-0-8156-3245-0

Library of Congress Cataloging-in-Publication Data

Sternlicht, Sanford V.
    [Reader's guide to modern Irish drama]
    Modern Irish drama : W.B. Yeats to Marina Carr / Sanford Sternlicht. — 2nd ed.
        p. cm.
    Previous ed.: A Reader's Guide to modern Irish drama, c1998.
    Includes bibliographical references and index.
    ISBN 978-0-8156-3245-0 (pbk. : alk. paper)
    1. English drama—Irish authors—History and criticism—Handbooks, manuals, etc.
    2. English drama—20th century—History and criticism—Handbooks, manuals, etc.
    3. English drama—19th century—History and criticism—Handbooks, manuals, etc.
    4. Ireland—In literature—Handbooks, manuals, etc.   I. Title.
    PR8789.S743 2010
    822'.91099417—dc22   2010019347

Manufactured in the United States of America

Contents

Preface

THE GENESIS OF THIS BOOK resulted from my teaching modern Irish drama at Syracuse University and at Trinity College, Dublin, for many summers under the auspices of the Syracuse University Ireland Program. In teaching these courses, I found that excellent play anthologies were available, but that there was no up-to-date handbook in print that satisfactorily provided the information necessary to support the course and help students understand the background to modern Irish drama and the scope of this great, ongoing artistic, cultural, and intellectual achievement of which the Irish people and Irish Americans are so justifiably proud.

I believe students of modern Irish drama as well as that part of the general reading public in the English-speaking world who have come to enjoy the fine plays of Brian Friel, Frank McGuinness, Marina Carr, Sebastian Barry, Martin McDonagh, Conor McPherson, and other Irish playwrights at work today want and need to know certain aspects of Irish history, especially from the early years of the twentieth century until now. Thus, I discuss the significance of the Irish Literary Revival, the story of the Irish National Theatre Society—which produced plays at the theater affectionately known as the Abbey, one of the great national theaters in the Western world—the general history of Irish drama and theater, and the achievements of the most significant Irish dramatists of the twentieth century. The volume also introduces the outstanding Irish plays of the modern and contemporary period.

Acknowledgments

MANY IRISH AND AMERICAN academics and playwrights have helped with this book, and I thank them all. I especially wish to thank Christopher Fitz-Simon, critic, theater historian, director, and actor, who is so very deserving of the esteem and affection that his peers and I have for him; Christopher Murray of University College, Dublin; Clive Geraghty of the Abbey Acting Company; Roger Hallas of Syracuse University, whose expertise in film studies aided in the construction of the filmography; and all my other colleagues in the English Department of Syracuse University who over the span of twenty-nine years have always made me feel that I am part of a proud, purposeful, and distinguished intellectual adventure.

Much support also came from Mark Weimer and other librarians of Bird Library at Syracuse University. I am grateful for support from Brian Calhoun-Bryant and Lisa Hanley of the College of Arts and Sciences Computer Services. But most of all I am much indebted to my life partner, Mary Beth Hinton, a fine editor whose advice, skills, and patience helped make this book possible.

PART ONE

Backgrounds

1

Early Irish History

CONTEMPORARY IRISH SOCIETY is a moving point on a continuum of evolving, superseding, incorporating cultures created by migration, conquest, colonization, imperial domination, religious and racial conflict and prejudice, and an overriding belief in a people's coherence, unity, and destiny. This destiny began with the aboriginal settlers of prehistoric Ireland who crossed the land bridge from what is now Scotland some ten thousand years ago and who were followed by Neolithic herders and then by farmers six thousand years ago—the latter clearing vast tracts of arable land out of the ubiquitous forests and building the great passage tombs such as Newgrange. In the Bronze Age (4000 to 3000 B.C.), the Beaker people brought metallurgy to Ireland, and they were followed in the third century B.C. by the most westerly expansion of the Celts and the Iron Age.

Celtic civilization created an heroic epoch, using Irish, the native Celtic language of Ireland (sometimes referred to as Gaelic or Irish Gaelic) to produce the first vernacular literature of western Europe and a glorious high culture. Although waxing and waning over the centuries, this culture remains an inspiration, a foundation, an architectonic, and the pride of contemporary Irish life.

The imperial Romans in Britain knew about Ireland but chose not to invade an island noted for its fierce warriors and rapacious pirates because they had enough difficulty with the unconquered Celtic Britons and Picts surrounding the perimeter of Britannia. When Rome's decline accelerated in the fifth century A.D., and as

3

the legions protecting Roman Britain were withdrawn, Irish and Germanic raiders began to plunder the disintegrating colony. A young, Romanized, Christian Celt named Patricius was captured by Irish slavers and taken across the Irish Sea. After servitude as a shepherd in Ireland, he made his way to the Continent for ordination as a priest and then returned to the land of his former captors as one of Christianity's first missionaries.

In the next century, the great Irish monasteries such as Armagh, St. Kevin's Glendalough, and St. Columba's Iona in the Hebrides off Scotland were founded. These monasteries flourished and, through the scribes' dedication and perseverance, preserved Roman and Greek literature. Thus, with the conversion of the pagan Germans, Goths, Franks, and Vandals, and with the extension of the Irish monastic movement to Britain and the Continent, classical culture was reintroduced to western Europe; Christianity was revitalized; and an intellectual, philosophical, ecclesiastic bulwark was built that helped the West to withstand the onslaught of Islam from the east and south later in the Middle Ages.

Celtic Ireland after St. Patrick was Christian and princely. Possessed of relative peace and surplus food production, it consequently could support a high culture. Many warrior chiefs gave fealty to the kings of the four traditional provinces: Ulster, Leinster, Munster, and Connaught. A titular high king, crowned at Tara, eventually reigned loosely over all. Then the first of the historical invasions began.

The Viking terror commenced in A.D. 795, and a partial Scandinavian occupation remained in effect for more than two hundred years, resulting in Ireland's isolation from continental Christian culture. It also led to the founding of Ireland's first cities: Dublin, Cork, Limerick, and others. The great high king Brian Boru, who reigned from 1002 to 1014, contained the Vikings and their Irish allies in Leinster and died victorious in battle at Clontarf.

But next came the Normans from Wales in 1169 under Strongbow. He was supported by the English king Henry II, to whom most Irish kings and bishops submitted, and Ireland began eight hundred years of conflict with England, a struggle that in Northern Ireland has only just ended.

Again and again over the centuries, civil wars and rebellions brought English troops to subdue the Irish populace and to lay waste the land. The Tudor and Stuart governments began the plantation system in Ulster to pacify the rebellious North in what was in reality the first English colony. They moved Protestant colonists from England and Scotland into the towns and onto the land, displacing the native Irish, most of whom had resisted the Reformation and remained loyal to the Church of Rome.

When both the Catholic South and Loyalist Ulster rebelled against the Puritan Commonwealth government of England, Oliver Cromwell arrived in Ireland in 1649, destroying Drogheda and Wexford, massacring much of their populations, and then banishing Catholic nobles and landowners to the remote West.

The Restoration of the British monarchy brought peace to Ireland, but it also saw continued anti-Catholic repression. In 1688, the Glorious Revolution in England deposed the Catholic king James II, and the next year he arrived in Ireland to fight his Protestant successor, William III, for the English Crown. Defeated in 1690 at the battle of the Boyne, an event still celebrated by Northern Irish Protestants to this day, James fled to France, and with the final defeat of his many loyal Catholic supporters at Aughrim in 1691, the fate of the Irish was sealed, and they were to be ruled by a Protestant England and the Protestant Ascendancy for the next 230 years.

The infamous Penal Laws—restrictions on Catholics' religious freedom, participation in public life, and inheritance rights as well as on their rights to vote, bear arms, receive higher education, and own land or even a horse—were enacted early in the eighteenth century. Although a barely tolerated unofficial religion, Catholicism was embraced by the vast majority of the Irish people, who in the course of the century slowly undermined many of the provisions of the Penal Laws. The impetus for equality and political freedom for all Irish people began its historical two-pronged assault on colonial rule and privilege: legislation and militant action. Inspired by the French Revolution, Wolfe Tone led the unsuccessful revolt of the United Irishmen in 1798, which was followed in 1803 by the even less successful rebellion led by Robert Emmet.

To obtain greater control of the country for both London and the Irish Protestant Ascendancy, the Irish Parliament in Dublin was dissolved with the Act of Union in 1800, and Dublin, once the second-largest city of the British Empire, began a long decline. The Act of Union was a setback for those Irish people, Catholic and Protestant alike, who dreamed of an independent Ireland or at least Home Rule. But Catholic emancipation by peaceful means was under way, led by Daniel O'Connell, "the Liberator." Just before the 1798 Wolfe Tone revolt, Roman Catholics obtained the right to vote and other civil rights. Then, in 1829, Catholics were permitted to hold seats in the Parliament in London. Later, in 1869, the Church of Ireland (Anglican) was disestablished, and the Irish Protestant bishops lost their seats in the British House of Lords.

The great watershed event in nineteenth-century Irish history that has had a lasting effect on world history and has scarred the Irish psyche was the famine of 1845–48, brought about by the combination of the potato blight, successive crop failures of that staple of the Irish peasant diet, and the British government's unwillingness to implement massive, practical, and timely relief efforts—actions that would have been antithetical to the laissez-faire economic principles of early capitalism. "The Great Hunger," as it is commonly referred to, resulted over time in the loss of nearly one-half of Ireland's pre-famine population of eight million through starvation, disease, and emigration. The present-day existence of large Irish communities in the United States, Canada, Australia, New Zealand, and elsewhere is largely owing to that terrible event. Another legacy is the widely held belief among many Irish people that the government in London did little to relieve starvation because of racist attitudes toward the poor, Catholic, Irish-speaking peasants of western Ireland, a population that the British government seemed to be content to be rid of, one way or another.

Another armed rising failed in the year of failed revolutions, 1848, and the nationalists of the Young Ireland movement faded away. A decade later the Irish Republican Brotherhood and the Fenian Brotherhood were formed to take up the cause of Irish freedom from Great Britain. The Fenians failed in their rising of 1867. A legislative tack was then tried again, and Home Rule, tenants' rights, and land reform became the political road to equality and the hope of eventual full emancipation. Charles Stewart Parnell became head of the Irish Parliamentary Party in 1881, bringing Ireland close to Home Rule in the Gladstone governments, but he tragically was disgraced and dismissed because of a divorce scandal. When the nineteenth century ended, most Irish Catholics were determined to achieve some degree of independence from Britain, but most of the Irish Protestants of the North, still loyal to the British Crown, were equally determined to remain in the United Kingdom of Great Britain and Ireland.

2

The Century of Destiny

POSITIONS HARDENED DRAMATICALLY with the coming of the twentieth century. Sinn Fein was established under Arthur Griffith in 1908, and three illegal armies were formed in 1913: the Ulster Volunteer Force in the North and the Irish Citizens Army and the Irish Volunteers in the South. The island was racked with labor strikes when in 1914 Home Rule for Ireland was disastrously put off until the cessation of World War I, when it was to be implemented after the peace treaty, with one parliament for Northern Ireland and another for the rest of the country. But the nationalists considered this compromise to be coming too late, and in the fateful year 1916 men from the Irish Revolutionary Brotherhood and the Irish Citizens Army, led by the poet Patrick Pearse and the labor union leader James Connolly, proclaimed the Irish Republic in Dublin on 24 April and fought the British army for five days. The British army's subsequent drawn-out execution of fifteen Republican prisoners from the Easter Rising shocked much of the world and galvanized the Irish majority in support of full independence from Britain even as thousands of Irishmen from Ulster and from the South were dying for Britain in the trenches of France and Belgium.

In December 1918, Republicans were victorious in general elections. They convened their own parliament, the Dail Eireann, in Dublin in January 1919 while the American-born Eamon de Valera, sole surviving commander in the Easter Rising and later prime minister and then president of Ireland, toured America in an attempt to obtain support for Irish claims at the Versailles Peace Conference. The Anglo-Irish War, also known as the Irish War of Independence, broke out at the same time, with the result that the occupation forces instituted martial law; ambushes, atrocities, and burnings marked a savage guerrilla war between Republicans under the brilliant tactician Michael Collins, on the one side, and the Royal Irish Constabulary and the notorious Black and Tans, a paramilitary force of former British soldiers, on the other, attempting on orders from London to terrorize the Irish into submission. Then Collins and his motorized flying squads and urban guerrillas were victorious, and the war-weary British finally requested a peace conference in 1921.

In 1922, the Dail approved the Anglo-Irish Treaty providing for the partition of Ireland into the Irish Free State (so called because the British government could not stomach the name "Republic of Ireland") in the South and Ulster in the North, with the latter remaining a part of the United Kingdom. The Irish Civil War ensued as antitreaty Republicans, Sinn Fein, with de Valera as their political leader, fought the new government army and were defeated; General Michael Collins was killed late in the conflict. The new state was thus tragically born in the blood of those who had fought together against the British but were now killing each other. Although hostilities finally ceased in 1923, the now illegal underground Irish Republican Army (IRA) continued to negate the terms of the treaty in hopes of forcing the British out of Northern Ireland.

Deciding to take the legislative route once more, de Valera left Sinn Fein in 1926 to found a new political party, Fianna Fail, and became head of government in 1932, first banning and eventually proscribing the IRA by 1936. Under a new constitution, the Irish Free State became Eire in 1937. As World War II broke out, Eire declared neutrality, and de Valera skillfully managed to keep the country out of the war despite Anglo-American pressure and the German bombing of Dublin. But because of de Valera's outdated economic and social policies, Ireland did not participate fully in the postwar European recovery.

In 1949, the Irish Republic was declared with the hope and intention of bringing internal peace to the island, but in the 1950s and 1960s the IRA continued its sporadic harassment of Great Britain and Northern Ireland, and the Ulster government allowed economic discrimination and occasional intimidation of its Catholic minority. In 1955, Ireland joined the United Nations, and in 1961 it tried but failed to be admitted to the European Economic Community. It was not until 1973 that Ireland was finally added to the European Union.

Set up to fight discrimination in 1967, the Northern Irish Civil Rights Association signaled a new militancy for the Catholic minority in Ulster, and the "Troubles" began the next year, lasting until the truce of 1994, which stood for only eighteen months. The years between 1968 and 1994 saw the assassinations of British officials and soldiers, IRA bombing campaigns in Britain and Northern Ireland, hunger strikes by IRA members in prison, and Loyalist opposition to possible Anglo-Irish agreements. Two of the worst events occurred in 1972: Bloody Sunday, when British soldiers shot to death fourteen nationalist marchers; and Bloody Friday, when an IRA bomb killed eleven people in Belfast.

But Eire moved on. The Roman Catholic Church's "special position" was eliminated from the Constitution. Mary Robinson became the first female president of Ireland in 1991. A referendum in 1995 permitted the introduction of divorce into Irish society for the first time since 1925. President Robinson was succeeded by another female president, Mary McAleese, in 1997.

To the relief of many millions of people in Ireland, Britain, and the United States—in fact, the vast Irish diaspora—the Good Friday Agreement of 10 April 1998 initiated a momentum toward peace in Northern Ireland that slowly led to a complete cessation of hostilities and, in 2007, a power-sharing government in the North.

Membership in the European Union helped the Republic of Ireland economically, and the country became more prosperous than it had ever been in its long history. With an outstanding educational system, some of the most fertile land in Europe, close connections with America and the rest of Europe, burgeoning high-tech industries, the youngest population in Europe, and a progressive immigration policy, Ireland moved into the twenty-first century with high hopes and great expectations.

Beginning in late 2007, however, Ireland, like all industrial nations, was stunned by the deepening recession brought about by unconscionable greed in financial institutions, unwise speculation, and the collapse of an enormous housing-price bubble. Unemployment rose dramatically as foreign-owned industries closed their Ireland operations, resulting in an exodus of guest workers and the emigration of young Irish people once more.

3

The Literary Tradition

THE CELTIC REVIVAL AND THE CELTIC TWILIGHT

With Catholic emancipation in the nineteenth century, the Irish people began to look back on their medieval cultural inheritance—the literature and art of the early Christian era—and to reconstruct the past in fine and applied art. Most significant, a renewed pride in the ancient tongue, Irish, revived the use and study of the language and probably saved it from extinction. In music, the sentimental and patriotic lyrics and scores of Thomas Moore contributed to the Celtic Revival, as did the poetry of James Clarence Mangan and the poetry and translations of Samuel Ferguson. The Gaelic League, founded in 1893, promulgated the teaching of the Irish language and, by inaugurating Irish festivals of singing, dancing, piping, fiddling, and poetry recitals, counteracted the feelings of inferiority of many native Irish speakers, who had been indoctrinated into believing that English was the superior tongue and that English culture was more sublime, advanced, and of greater value than Irish culture.

William Butler Yeats—Ireland's greatest poet and arguably, of course, the foremost poet of the English language in the twentieth century—employed the phrase "the Celtic Twilight" as the title of his book of Irish folklore published in 1893, using it to describe the literary and artistic mood in Ireland in the last decade of the nineteenth century and the first decade of the twentieth, a romantic mood of shadowy mysticism and mournfulness. This misty view of ancient Ireland—an Irish version of Pre-Raphaelitism—may have been inspired by Matthew Arnold's 1867 Oxford lecture "On the Study of Celtic Literature." Although the realists and modernists who came after Yeats reacted against and denigrated Yeats and his followers' flowery, self-referential, pastoral, and heavily imagistic poetry, the international public loved this verse and pseudo-archaic tales for the beauty of their language and the power of their sentiments.

THE IRISH LITERARY RENAISSANCE

The Irish Literary Revival, or Irish Literary Renaissance, a phenomenon coterminous with the Celtic Twilight, grew out of the historical writings of Standish O'Grady, which celebrated the Heroic Age of Ireland for a people thirsty for heroes and heroines. It also was influenced greatly by the nationalist fervor instilled in young writers by that old Fenian John O'Leary, who was released from an English prison in 1884 and returned to Ireland to help educate the younger generation and build an Irish consciousness.

Yeats founded the Irish Literary Society of London in 1891 and the National Literary Society in Dublin the next year. He was indeed a great *founder*—founding the Dublin Hermetic Society first in 1885, then the Irish Literary Theatre in 1897, the Irish National Theatre Society in 1902, and the venerable Abbey Theatre in 1904. Indeed, Yeats was the true father of the Irish Literary Renaissance.

Although the writers of the Irish Literary Renaissance worked almost exclusively in the English language, their English was in various ways influenced, inflected, and subverted by underlying Irish linguistic patterns and lexicon. Their work was a remarkable outpouring of world-class literature from a small nation with a tiny population, afloat on the western edge of Europe. This period of high creativity has been given widely differing dates; in a way, the renaissance continues, for little Ireland is very big indeed when it comes to internationally recognized writers (four of them won the

Nobel Prize for Literature: Yeats in 1923, George Bernard Shaw in 1925, Samuel Beckett in 1969, and Seamus Heaney in 1995). I offer the dates from 1885 to 1939, the year of Yeats's death, as workable and useful for the Irish Literary Renaissance, for in the sense of dominating influence Yeats *was* the renaissance.

The writers of the period form a pantheon of literary achievement in poetry, fiction, and drama. Besides Yeats, they include James Joyce (of course), Lady Gregory, Edith Sommerville and Violet Martin (Sommerville and Ross), John Millington Synge, George Moore, Katherine Tynan, George Fitzmaurice, Sean O'Casey, AE (George William Russell), Padraic Colum, Thomas MacDonagh, Joseph Campbell, James Stephens, Austin Clarke, Frank O'Connor, Peadar O'Donnell, Sean O'Faolain, Patrick Kavanagh, Liam O'Flaherty, Lord Dunsany, Seamus O'Kelly, George Shiels, Lennox Robinson, Brinsley MacNamara, Elizabeth Bowen, and the young Samuel Beckett, among others.

In the period of the Irish Literary Renaissance, Irish writing moved from nineteenth-century romanticism into early-twentieth-century modernism, making a magnificent contribution to what became the dominant literary high style of the century of world war, revolution, genocide, population explosion, and technological advance beyond the wildest dreams of past humanity.

A SILVER AGE

Irish writers continued to show remarkable creativity and to hold a significant position in the wide world of belletristic writing during the second half of the twentieth century, and their descendants have carried the torch into the twenty-first. It is not just Nobel laureates who are recognized internationally, but also many other excellent writers. Dramatists Brian Friel, Marina Carr, Martin McDonagh, and Conor McPherson command a world stage. Poets, other playwrights, and fiction writers of great note include Mary

Lavin, Iris Murdoch, Joyce Carey, Louis MacNeice, Michael J. Molloy, Denis Johnston, Michael McLaverty, Benedict Kiley, Brendan Behan, Patrick Kavanagh, Thomas Kinsella, John B. Keane, Eugene McCabe, Thomas Kilroy, Tom Murphy, Tom Mac Intrye, Michael Longley, John McGahern, John Montague, Brendan Kinnelly, Derek Mahon, William Trevor, Brian Moore, Jennifer Johnston, Edna O'Brien, Derek Mahon, Julia O'Faolain, Eavan Boland, John McGahern, Bernard McLaverty, Eilean ni Chuilleanain, Michael O Siadhail, Hugh Maxton, Medbh McGuckian, Nuala ni Dhomhnaill, Paul Muldoon, Frank McGuinness, John Banville, Roddy Doyle, Maeve Binchy, James Plunkett, Christy Brown, Paul Muldoon, Brendan Kennelly, Richard Murphy, Seamus Deane, Pat McCabe, Colm Tóibin, and, of course, Seamus Heaney.

4

The Irish Theater

THEATER CAME TO IRELAND in the Middle Ages with the Anglo-Norman invaders. Mystery plays, which were based on the Bible, and morality plays, which served as dramatized allegorical sermons, were performed in the towns under the auspices of the church and the guilds on holidays such as Whitsuntide and Corpus Christi. Because Ireland remained mostly Catholic even after Henry VIII brought the Reformation to England and to those areas of Ireland under English control, the religious drama continued unabated until Oliver Cromwell's assault on Irish civilization.

Ireland's first professional theater, the Werburgh Street Theatre, was opened in Dublin, near Dublin Castle, in 1637, but it lasted only four years. There, the first play on a purely Irish subject, *St. Patrick for Ireland,* written by resident dramatist James Shirley, was performed in 1639.

In 1692, after the restoration of Charles II to the English throne, Dublin's Theatre Royal, or Smock Alley, opened, and once again Irish playwrights had a local venue. But like the Werburgh Theatre, Smock Alley, located in what is now the Temple Bar district of Dublin, was a provincial stage where the fare was primarily imports from London.

In the late seventeenth century and on into the eighteenth century, Irish writers frequently moved to London to try to make their fortunes. One of the most notable was William Congreve, who left Dublin for London in 1689 at the age of nineteen, and his four

16

great comedies—*The Old Bachelor, The Double Dealer, Love for Love,* and *The Way of the World*—were first performed there.

Derry-born George Farquhar began his theatrical career as a Smock Alley actor and then moved to London, where his plays *Love and a Bottle, The Constant Couple, Sir Harry Wildhair, The Recruiting Officer,* and *The Beaux' Stratagem*—his masterpiece—were produced with varying success.

Many other Irish playwrights followed Congreve and Farquhar across the Irish Sea, and at the same time the great actors of the English stage, including David Garrick, came over to perform in Dublin. In the mid–eighteenth century, the multitalented Oliver Goldsmith, who had left Ireland to seek literary fame in London, achieved theater immortality by writing what is arguably the greatest English-language comedy of the enlightened century, *She Stoops to Conquer.*

The Derry-born actor Charles Macklin starred in famous productions of Shakespeare and other plays on the London stage, becoming in addition the first Irish-born actor-manager. The second, remaining in Dublin to manage Smock Alley, was Thomas Sheridan, who earned actors' undying affection by banning the practice of allowing members of the audience to sit on the stage and by actually paying actors contracted salaries! His son, the sharp-witted Richard Brinsley Sheridan, wrote two masterpieces for the late-eighteenth-century London stage: *The Rivals* and *School for Scandal.* The famous London actor-manager William Macready was also an Irishman.

The late seventeenth century and the eighteenth century clearly established that the Irish genius was for comedy. This connection appears as true today as it was then.

In the nineteenth century, the great Irish actors were Barry Sullivan and Tyrone Power, ancestor of the American film star of the 1930–50 period. The first Tyrone Power perfected the stage-Irish character, a comic caricature that now seems as painful and out of place as a racial joke. The most commercially successful Irish dramatist of the nineteenth century was the prolific and internationally famous writer of melodramas Dion Boucicault, most admired in Ireland for his sentimental trilogy *Colleen Bawn, Arrah na Pogue,* and *The Shaughraun.*

From the eighteenth century through the nineteenth century, theaters in Europe grew larger and thus less intimate, in part to accommodate larger audiences (and earn more money for the managers) and in part because of the emphasis on spectacular melodramas, opera, Shakespearean productions, and various multiscene extravaganzas. The first new theaters in Dublin were on Aungier, Capel, Fishamble, and Crowe streets. Today, two nineteenth-century theaters still survive in Dublin: the Gaiety and the Olympia. Belfast's Grand Opera House, severely damaged in an IRA attack, has been restored to its former glory. Almost all of the early theaters in smaller Irish towns have been either abandoned or torn down, however.

Beyond question, Ireland's great nineteenth-century contribution to world drama was the work of the incomparable Oscar Wilde, perhaps the wittiest person who ever put pen to paper. Born in Dublin, Wilde went to Oxford after Trinity College, Dublin. Later, in London, as a leader of the Aesthetic Movement, he became a controversial but much appreciated public figure who enjoyed outraging conservative society with his wit and his seemingly *Yellow Book* magazine decadent lifestyle. His superb plays still grace the boards of theaters everywhere, including *Lady Windermere's Fan, A Woman of No Importance, An Ideal Husband,* and the greatest English-language comedy—indeed, play—of the nineteenth century, *The Importance of Being Earnest.* As is well known, Wilde's career ended in sexual scandal and his life, alas, in bitter exile.

Born only two years after Wilde and in the same city was the long-lived, laughter-loving propagandist and social theorist George Bernard Shaw, the second Irishman (after Yeats) to win the Nobel Prize for Literature. Shaw delighted audiences everywhere in the

English-speaking world with his thesis comedies that explored problems of gender, poverty, religion, war, and class as Henrik Ibsen did in the genre of tragedy. Shaw's legacy to world drama has proved worthy of a festival devoted to his work, and his major plays—*Arms and the Man, The Devil's Disciple, Candida, Man and Superman, The Doctor's Dilemma, Pygmalion,* and *Saint Joan*—are continually performed.

Also of great significance is Shaw's one great "Irish" play, *John Bull's Other Island,* written for Yeats and the early Abbey in 1904 but then initially declined by Yeats (who it must be said never had much sympathy for Shavian thesis comedy) and thus first produced in London instead of Dublin. The play might have been too hot a political potato for the fledgling theater to handle, or perhaps the large-cast, multiscene play was beyond the company's and the tiny theater's capabilities at so early a date. The Abbey finally put on *John Bull's Other Island* in 1914, and it became a perennial favorite in Dublin for many years, never ceasing to provoke heated discourse. The play is a favorite of mine because, besides its wicked wit, its satire on English-Irish relations seems perennially current. I describe *John Bull's Other Ireland* more fully later on.

The great national theater enterprise and modern Irish drama and theater began with the founding of the Irish Literary Theatre in 1897 by Yeats, Edward Martyn, and Lady Isabella Augusta Gregory—all playwrights. Yeats wrote poetic drama from his background in Irish mythology and in accordance with the principles and practices of the French symbolists. Lady Gregory employed her knowledge of and affection for the Irish peasants who lived around her home in Gort, near Galway, and she found her dramatic models in French comedy. Martyn was a disciple of Ibsen and a writer of problem plays and social drama.

The Irish Literary Theatre began producing in 1899 with performances of Yeats's symbolic, medieval, poetic drama *The Countess Cathleen* and Martyn's problem play on landlord-tenant relations, *The Heather Field*. The venue was the Antient Concert Hall Rooms, a concert hall seating eight hundred. Other productions were put on in the Gaiety, a grand Victorian theater. In 1902, the Irish Literary Theatre, now called the National Dramatic Society, performed Yeats's fiercely nationalistic *Cathleen ni Houlihan* and AE's (George Russell) dreamy *Deirdre* in the three-hundred-seat St. Theresa's Hall.

In 1903, the National Dramatic Society became the Irish National Theatre Society, and its theater, familiarly known as "the Abbey" because of its location on Lower Abbey Street, opened in 1904 with a performance of Yeats's mythological *On Baile's Strand* and Lady Gregory's peasant comedy *Spreading the News*. The Irish National Theatre Society at the Abbey went on to become and remain one of Europe's most important national repertory theaters, like the Moscow Art Theater. The Abbey is a cultural jewel that is not only a source of great pride for the Irish people, but also the envy of many nations.

The Abbey's main mission remains primarily but not exclusively to produce plays by Irish playwrights on Irish themes. It has always been to a very large extent a writers' theater. With its inception, ordinary people, peasant farmers, city workers, fisherfolk, back-country people, itinerants, small merchants, the poor, the sick, and the blind would find a place and a voice on the Irish stage, whereas the foolish and embarrassing, shifty, hot-tempered, lazy, conniving, often drunken, comic "stage Irishman," speaking in a ludicrously exaggerated accent, was banished except for in historical revivals of early works.

Shortly after the Abbey's founding and initial successes, rival companies in Dublin were set up. Most notable was the Irish Theatre Company, 1914–20, under Edward Martyn, who had broken with his fellow Abbey directors, but none of the early rivals survived.

In the beginning, the Irish National Theatre Society attempted plays in the Irish language, such as the folk comedies of Douglas Hyde (who was later the first president of Ireland under the Constitution of 1937), but with limited success, so most of Ireland's

dramatic contributions have been in English. Much later, Taibhd-
hearc na Gaillimhe, the Irish-language theater located in Galway,
continued the tradition of performances in Irish, but it had greater
success with translations from other languages. Gael-Linn in Dublin in the 1950s produced Irish-language plays to encourage use of
Irish Gaelic. Its greatest success was in 1958 with Brendan Behan's
1958 play *An Giall (The Hostage)*.

Yeats's inspiration and Lady Gregory's managerial skills and
diplomacy sustained the Abbey in its infancy and early adolescence.
Of course, the timely infusion of money from the English heiress
Annie Horniman, a friend of Yeats, proved decisive in the beginning. Yeats and Lady Gregory brought John Millington Synge to
the Abbey. Synge's superb one-acters *In the Shadow of the Glen* and
Riders to the Sea and his full-length masterpieces *Playboy of the Western World* and *The Well of the Saints* established him as the leading
Abbey dramatist in its early years. Yeats and Gregory also discovered
the youthful Padraic Colum, whose three plays written in the first
decade of the twentieth century—*The Fiddler's House, The Land,*
and *Thomas Muskerry*—helped bring the peasant play into prominence and obtained a popular audience for the Abbey Theatre and
the new Irish drama in general. The country plays of William Boyle
and George Fitzmaurice also added to the growth of this audience.

The Abbey needed good actors, and it grew its own, starting
with the former amateurs Frank and William Fay, who as perform-
ers and directors turned the company and the theater into a professional organization. The early-twentieth-century Irish stage was
also graced by Florence Farr, Barry Fitzgerald, Sarah Allgood, Molly
Allgood, F. J. McCormack, Moira O'Neill, and Fred O'Donovan.
The first two mentioned became world famous through American
film. Jack McGowran, Patrick Magee, Cyril Cussack, Milo O'Shea,
Siobhán McKenna, and the old perennial Shakespearean Anew
McMaster later added luster to the Irish stage and in some cases to
the international cinema.

Ireland's great playwright in the years between the world wars was Dublin-born Sean O'Casey, whom Lady Gregory brought into the theater. His reputation rests on the magnificent tragicomic historic trilogy of the Irish Free State's birth trauma: *The Shadow of a Gunman, Juno and the Paycock,* and *The Plough and the Stars.* Other popular Irish playwrights of the period include George Shiels, St. John Ervine, Teresa Deevey, and Lennox Robinson—the latter associated with the Abbey for fifty years as a playwright, manager, and director. In the 1920s, the actor, designer, and playwright Micheál MacLiammóir and the actor-director Hilton Edwards founded the privately funded Dublin Gate Theatre, one of Ireland's longest-surviving theater enterprises. The Gate has achieved world renown through the quality of its productions, which emphasize international classics by such modern dramatists as Henrik Ibsen (the founder of modern drama), Eugene O'Neill, and Jean Cocteau as well as works by Irish playwrights. The friendly rivalry between the Abbey and the Gate over the decades, although some would deny its existence, has been to the great advantage of Irish culture.

The old Abbey Theatre was a converted concert hall that had belonged to the Mechanics' Institute; for a lobby or foyer and business offices, it had an old bank building that in a yet earlier life had been the Dublin morgue. In 1951, however, the Abbey burned, and the ruins were torn down. The hall had been loved by the public and hated by the company. The Abbey's proscenium had been only twenty-one feet wide and fifteen feet deep, which meant there was little room for backdrops or shutters and practically no space to build. Most plays produced there consequently required only a single set, often a room in a farmer's cottage in the West Country.

For fifteen years after the theater burned and was torn down, the Abbey company performed in the old Queen's Theatre near Trinity College, now demolished and lamented, where productions were often lacking in distinction, to a large extent because of a paucity of government financial support. But other companies in Dublin and other Irish cities took up the challenge of performing exciting new work. Brendan Behan's *The Quare Fellow* was turned down by the Abbey company but was produced in 1954 at the Pike Theatre Club, founded by one of Ireland's finest directors, Alan Simpson, among others. The Pike also presented the first Irish production of Beckett's *Waiting for Godot* in 1955. At last, the new Abbey Theatre opened in 1966 on the original site in a relatively modest but quite functional building designed by Michael Scott. Today plans are being made to remodel the thirty-one-year-old theater extensively.

Northern Ireland developed its own theater traditions, especially in Belfast, where, beginning in 1902, the Ulster Literary Theatre, led by Bulmer Hobson, also encouraged Irish dramatists, deriving its inspiration from the Irish Literary Theatre in the South. After thirty years, it was succeeded by the Ulster Group Theatre, which had a twenty-year run. The Lyric Theatre is currently the leading venue for drama in Belfast, although it seems that its fare is generally more British and international than Irish. But Belfast, like Dublin, is a theater town. Several smaller companies are continually mounting exciting Irish plays and international hits; Charabanc and Dubblejoint are outstanding examples. Belfast productions are often seen in Dublin and North America.

Derry's groundbreaking Field Day Theatre Company, now out of existence, is forever enshrined in Irish theater history for introducing Brian Friel's *Translations* to an admiring world in 1980, its premier season. Playing all of Ireland and Wales, Scotland, and England, too, the new Irish Theatre Company brought Irish plays and world classics to provincial cities as well as the capitals from 1974 to 1982. The company included several of Ireland's most talented modern directors, including Joe Dowling and Christopher Fitz-Simon.

From a largely Protestant upper-middle-class outer suburb and Trinity College emerged Samuel Beckett, arguably the greatest dramatist of the twentieth century. After Trinity, Beckett moved to France, eventually settling there, surviving anti-German underground action in World War II as a member of the French Resistance, writing in French, and translating his work into English. His existential masterpieces of the 1950s and early 1960s—*Waiting for Godot, Endgame,* and *Happy Days*—profoundly affected and perhaps changed not only the theater of Western culture, but also the way human beings living in this culture perceive reality and contemplate their own lives. Performed in English, Beckett's plays, if done well, sound Irish and remind culturally aware audiences of Yeats and Synge.

Not as profound as Beckett but certainly making better newspaper copy was the irrepressible, beloved, heavy-drinking, and ultimately tragic Dublin-born IRA fighter Brendan Behan, whose reputation was established with the Pike Theatre's production of *The Quare Fellow* in 1954. On that play and *The Hostage,* his reputation as a playwright rests. It is interesting to note that Beckett and Behan were writing their major plays at about the same time. How different and yet how similar their values are! Behan is political (an Irish Republican), and Beckett seems not to be. But, of course, Beckett, as a Marxist ideologue tempered by existential compassion and ennui, is the ultimate political being. Both of these Irish playwrights have a basically seriocomic weltanschauung—that life is a funny tragedy. In fact, their Irishness unites them.

In the forefront of today's host of fine Irish dramatists stand Brian Friel, Frank McGuinness, Marina Carr, Martin McDonagh, and Conor McPherson. Friel's reputation was established with *Philadelphia, Here I Come!* (directed by Hilton Edwards) and solidified with worldwide performances of *Translations* and *Dancing at Lughnasa.* McGuinness's *Observe the Sons of Ulster Marching Towards the Somme* electrified audiences all over Ireland and Britain; his hostage drama *Someone Who'll Watch over Me* was especially moving for American audiences. Carr's *By the Bog of Cats* combines archetypal experience with modern feminism to engage women and men profoundly. McDonagh's macabre humor in West Country Irish settings has intrigued audiences everywhere. And McPherson's poignant and poetic dramas of stressed and lonely Irish people are everywhere admired.

Today the Irish theater appears very much alive and well, despite the closing of the Andrews Lane Theatre in Dublin. The Abbey, of course, has financial problems, but they are not new. More significant, the theater continues to produce artistic successes. It thrives on the mixture of Irish classics and selected modern and contemporary plays. The Abbey's smaller stage, the Peacock, showcases the performance of a seemingly endless stream of brilliant plays by younger, lesser-known dramatists who are at the beginning of very promising careers.

The Dublin Gate Theatre has added to its international reputation with enthusiastically received tours. The Gaiety Theatre delights a popular audience of Irish people and visitors. The Projects Arts Centre in Temple Bar provided a compatible venue for experimental new plays but has now closed. Several other professional and semiprofessional groups present Irish plays new and old, Shakespeare, Elizabethan and Jacobean drama, European and American plays, and experimental performance theater. The annual Dublin Theatre Festival provides a platform for new work. Dinner theaters are growing in number, and theater in the universities throughout Ireland is flourishing and providing trained artists for the Irish stage, television, and cinema.

In Belfast, as noted earlier, the Lyric and several small companies provide original, exciting, and excellent theater. Founded in 1975 in Galway by Garry Hynes, Mick Lally, and Marie Mullen, the Druid Theatre, through spirited productions of new Irish plays and Irish classics, has built a stellar reputation that has extended far beyond Ireland's shores. Other Irish cities have very successful repertory and producing companies, too, along with well-equipped, comfortable theaters. And the Irish community theater movement is enviable in its scope, enthusiasm, and quality.

In addition, Radio Telefís Eireann and the BBC, mighty cultural forces, have encouraged Irish theater artists of all types and have significantly helped to sustain and grow the audience for the Irish theater.

The world of scholarship has also embraced and supported Irish drama and theater. A steady flow of books and articles on Irish culture cascades from international presses and periodicals. Useful and informative Usenet newsgroups and sites focusing on Irish drama and theater abound on the Internet. The American Conference for Irish Studies, the International Association for the Study of Irish Literature, and Irish studies programs in American, British, and Canadian universities sustain interest in Irish drama and theater and provide a continuing international audience for both modern Irish plays and those that have and will be written in the postmodern era.

At the very beginning of the twentieth century, a handful of patriotic would-be playwrights and actors in a small country working in a makeshift theater created, to their own astonishment, one of history's great national repertory theaters and a dramatic tradition that is a wonder of modern culture. Irish theater today confidently anticipates a bright future.

PART TWO

Playwrights and Plays

5

A Thematic Introduction

NOT SURPRISINGLY, many themes weave their way in and out of the 115-year history of modern Irish drama. Most pervading is the theme of nationalism, first emphatically introduced by Yeats and in the 1920s turned into a subject of satire and derision by O'Casey (for which some never forgave him). Modern Irish drama evolved from the nationalistic movement at the turn of the twentieth century. It was conceived out of the energy and the ardor of those Irish writers who believed that the Irish nation was awaiting a rebirth as a self-governing people. Yeats called upon the ancient heroic past to provide thematic subjects for the new Irish drama, and Colum found heroism in peasant life and action in the recent past, such as in the Land War of the 1880s. One can reasonably argue that modern Irish nationalism came into being in part because of the fervor of the Anglo-Irish writers of the late nineteenth and early twentieth centuries, and it was under the leadership of poets that the Rising of 1916 occurred.

The great and ancient theme of Anglo-Irish conflict is somewhat muted in the present, pushed into the background by the related and derived theme of Unionist-Republican conflict, now seemingly abated, and by the fight for civil rights in Ulster. The Anglo-Irish struggle is now primarily a cultural one, with the smaller nation, physically cut off from its European cousins by that far larger and wealthier neighboring first cousin who stands between it and the rest of Europe and with whom there must somehow be a full rapprochement. Related to this theme is the theme of intermarriage between Catholics and Protestants, often expressed in tragic Romeo and Juliet scenarios.

But the peasant drama also had themes that did not play, so to speak, on the national political stage. These themes, close to the hearts and ever in the minds of ordinary people, included the painful problems of exile and emigration as they impacted family, community, and even nation; of leaving and sometimes returning; and of the devastating breaking of traditionally strong family ties. Although Ireland's chief export is no longer human talent, the latter theme is still current in the nation and in the wider Irish world—as witnessed, for example, by the continuing success of revivals of Friel's *Philadelphia, Here I Come!*

Then there are the marriage wars and the struggle of the young to overcome the impediments of arranged marriages when they desire to pursue their own destinies. There is also the struggle for land ownership and inheritance in a country where for centuries it was nearly impossible for a Roman Catholic peasant to own land. When land ownership was finally possible, the parcels acquired could not sustain the traditionally large families; second and third sons had to leave the farm and make their way in the wide world as best they could, and daughters were married off to any man who could support them.

The theme of poverty, of course, has persisted as long as the actuality. Another powerful theme is the breaking away from the father's power by his offspring, who seek through education and enterprise a life off the land and out of the clutches of the patriarchal family and the collaborating church. The themes focused on the past are, of course, eminently exportable because American, British, and commonwealth audiences, with their large percentage of citizens of Irish or partially Irish ancestry, are nostalgically curious about life, especially rural life, in the world of their great-grandparents.

Today in Ireland the archromantic, mythic, heroic theme is much out of fashion, and peasant life seems remote to a nation that is primarily city-dwelling and forward looking. To an Ireland now trying to dilute the legacy of a seemingly backward past, the ways of the old peasant now appear to be no longer pertinent and are even considered quaint—useful largely as the subject of satire or farce.

Related to the dramatic, historically and theatrically speaking, is the now fading theme of the disruption of rural life resulting from the migration to the cities in the post–World War II era. This theme is generally presented from the perspective of the new, young, city dweller who is simultaneously fascinated, happy, lonely, impressionable, rootless, and lost in his or her new environment.

The stagnation of provincial life caused by the inertia resulting from the crushing alliance of church, temporal power, and local hierarchy dedicated to maintaining the status quo in society has continued in Irish drama with little abatement since the beginning of the twentieth century. It is a consequence not only of colonialism, but also of the economically conservative de Valera era. This stagnation or at least the sense that it still persists, despite the church's loss of authority owing to persistent scandals, has caused some young people's incorrect perception that Irish culture is inadequate and inferior to that of other Western nations. This perception feeds a desire for imported values and culture, particularly from America and Britain. It is as if Ireland still stands as a poor neighbor between two wealthy ones who don't see her or regard her and are content to talk over her head. Postmodern Irish dramatists have made much of this perception.

A lighter perennial theme in Irish drama is the Irish people's love of taking flights of fancy, letting imagination have its head, reveling in fantasy and what might have been and yet might be—and telling it with gusto, of course.

On the very dark side, there is the theme of slanderous misogyny: women are predatory, prurient, and ever disrespectful or despising of their husbands, their lovers, and sometimes even their fathers. Counterbalancing this theme is that of the brutal, insensitive, sometimes drunken father and husband, politically and materially powerless, but the terror of the home. The current manifestation of this ever-present theme can be seen in the work of young, new women writers, who comprehend and express Irish women's dissatisfaction with their role in society, articulating that dissatisfaction by eschewing this violent history, recognizing the weakening of the traditional moral alliance between mother and priest against the father's economic and legal power, and evidencing disappointment in Irish men as faithful companions and adequate sexual partners.

Like most societies, Ireland is engaged in the business of reenvisioning and reimaging its history. Depicting those activities is continually a function of drama. Because theater is such a popular medium in Ireland, history revisited—particularly recent history— remains a major preoccupation among contemporary dramatists.

In the broadest terms, Irish drama in the twentieth century and beyond has followed two paths, the path of realism or naturalism and the path of expressionism. Despite the influence of Yeats's romanticism, lyricism, and mysticism, the Abbey Theatre has followed primarily the realistic path pioneered early in the century by Lady Gregory, Martyn, and Colum and continued with such early 1920s masterpieces as O'Casey's Anglo-Irish and Civil War trilogy—but not with his expressionistic *The Silver Tassie* (1929), which, like Denis Johnston's surrealistic *The Old Lady Says No!* (1929), was rejected by the Abbey. (Significantly, Johnston changed the title of his play to the one given here because someone wrote those words on his rejected manuscript—"the old lady" was Lady Gregory, of course.) Expressionist, surrealistic, darkly satirical, and sardonic plays found their venue for much of the twentieth century at the Gate, Peacock, and the Pike theaters as well as at little Off-Broadway-type theaters in Dublin, Belfast, London, and elsewhere.

These perennial Irish themes have served tragedy, comedy, melodrama, and farce. The Irish have always adored comedy, yet it is no wonder that Beckett, in *Endgame,* has Nell say: "Nothing is funnier than unhappiness."

6

The Founders

BORN ISABELLA AUGUSTA PERSSE, twelfth in a family of sixteen children, at Roxborough, County Galway, in the West of Ireland, and educated privately, Lady Gregory was a child of the Protestant Anglo-Irish Ascendancy, whose manorial estates in rural Ireland and the accompanying townhouses were sites of political unionism, authority, and gentility. But in childhood and adolescence, Augusta, as she was always called by family and friends, developed artistic sensibilities and grew sympathetic to the Republican views of many of the common people of the estates and the small towns and villages. Sean O'Casey, born in Dublin, was quite correct when, late in Lady Gregory's life, he wrote to her: "You can always walk with your head up. . . . [R]emember you had to fight against your birth into position and comfort, as others had to fight against their birth into hardship and poverty."

Lady Gregory read Fenian political tracts and collected folk ballads. As a young woman, she tried to help local farmers in their economic struggle with wholesalers and retailers of their produce. As a married woman, she wrote pamphlets supporting certain liberal Irish causes that were intended to ease British control, but she was against Home Rule for Ireland.

In 1880, Augusta Persse married Sir William Gregory and came to live at Coole Park, near Gort, County Galway. The mansion, surrounding park, and supporting farms became a place of inspiration and sustenance for many Irish writers because of Lady Gregory's generous patronage. Yeats came almost every summer to enjoy the park and the lake, the good food and conversation, and the opportunity to relax, think, and create. No wonder that when he chose a home for his bride and family to come to, he settled only a few miles away from Coole.

Sir William was a widower of sixty-three and Lady Gregory twenty-eight at the time of their marriage. She had suitors near her own age, but her mother had rejected them as not having enough social status for the family. The Gregorys had one child, Robert, much beloved by his mother, but he was killed in action with the Royal Flying Corps in 1918. One of Yeats's most famous poems, "An Irish Airman Foresees His Death," was written to try to comfort his grieving friend.

When Lady Gregory's husband died in 1892, she commenced to edit his autobiography for publication, and she wore black for the rest of her life. Most important, however, she served her apprenticeship as a writer in this dutiful work, developing a clear and fluid style. Also significant was her ability to make and keep friends whether they agreed with her political views or not. Lady Gregory studied Irish Gaelic with her son and became fluent in the language.

Finally, she began what became a major architectonic of her life as a writer: the collection and editing of West Country folklore and history, sometimes in the local Kiltartan Irish-English dialect. Her published works in this genre include *Poets and Dreamers* (1903), *A Book of Saints and Wonders* (1906), *The Kiltartan History Book* (1909), *The Kiltartan Wonder Book* (1910), and the two-volume *Visions and Beliefs in the West of Ireland* (1920). Of wider impact were *Cuchulain of Muirthemne* (1902) and *Gods and Fighting Men* (1904), in which she compiled, translated, and adapted the ancient Irish epics so that Ireland would have texts to stand next to

Malory's version of the Arthuriad, *Morte D'Arthur*, and the Welsh *Mabinogion*.

It is as a playwright and as a cofounder and guiding light of the Abbey Theatre that Lady Gregory will be best remembered. She wrote twenty-seven original plays, even though she was nearly fifty when she began playwriting professionally. Her reputation as a dramatist rests primarily on *Seven Short Plays* (1909) and a few other one-act and two-act plays. Her frequently performed comedies are *Spreading the News* (1905), *Hyacinth Halevy* (1906), and *The Jackdaw* (1909). *The Rising of the Moon* (1904), *The Workhouse Ward* (1909), and *The Gaol Gate* (1909) are popular one-act political plays. Her longer works—the folk history plays *Kincora* (1905), *Dervorgilla* (1907), and *Grania* (1912)—are little regarded today, as are the tragicomedies and a few late comedies.

Most significant, Lady Gregory secretly collaborated with Yeats on his early plays, including the famous politically inflammatory *Cathleen ni Houlihan* (1901). She was better than he at peasant dialogue and settings, and she wanted to support the young writer of whom she was so fond. She should be listed at least as coauthor in publications of this play.

Lady Gregory and the Abbey Theatre are forever linked in Irish cultural history. She cofounded the Irish National Theatre Society and its predecessors; encouraged, supported, and defended the first true genius of an Irish playwright of the twentieth century, John Millington Synge, against nationalists and censors in Ireland and America; discovered and encouraged that difficult genius Sean O'Casey; and was a lifelong supporter and best friend of Yeats. With magnificent adroitness she also kept the Abbey and the company safe from temperamental self-destruction, disastrous elitism, external censorship, political and ecclesiastical control, and Catholic-Protestant rivalry for some thirty years.

Augusta Gregory died at Coole on 22 May 1932. Ireland and the world are forever in her debt.

Plays

Lady Gregory's strengths as a playwright are in the genre of light comedy. Her short, humorous, peasant plays still have the power to entertain and delight audiences today and are frequently performed, especially by community and other amateur groups. At the beginning of the twentieth century, she mastered the art of reproducing natural speech and locating dramatic situations in the lives of the common people of Ireland's West. Perhaps an incentive for Lady Gregory was the perceived need to counteract the high seriousness and intense versification in those "literary" plays of Yeats that had limited audience appeal. After all, Lady Gregory had originally hoped that the new Irish theater company would tour rural Ireland, putting on plays for the people of the countryside, many of whom would not have seen a professional play previously. These relatively unsophisticated people would have related much more comfortably to the stage portraits of people like themselves than to portraits of ancient Celtic chieftains and war goddesses.

Lady Gregory is also skilled in creating simple plots. She is the inveterate storyteller, bringing a local yarn to life in a very basic, even primeval way—or, to use the American vernacular, "telling it like it is." She created the mythical village of Coon, based on the real Gort near her home, as the setting for many of her comedies. A modern reader or viewer might suppose that her naturalist renderings of village and peasant life in a humorous mode are manifestations of aristocratic condescension or colonial perspective: the kindly and sympathetic lady of the manor amused by the machinations of the lower classes or the natives. But I think that we witness in Gregory's comedy, tragicomedy, and miracle and mystery plays precisely what is valorized in her epic adaptations: a drive to establish a delineated Irish character, an Irish collective destiny, an Irish self-recognition, self-respect, and self-understanding.

Lady Gregory's comedies are woven about the themes of illusion and delusion as well as appearance versus reality. Characters are fooled, they deceive and trick each other, confusion causes further confusion, and things are never quite what they seem to observers within the plays. Confusion naturally leads to comic situations and farcical denouement. Hers is a gentle comedy of manners rather than an acerbic comedy of vice.

Twenty-Five (1903)

Twenty-Five is the story of Christy, a young man who immigrated to America, but who has returned to his native village with one hundred pounds saved, ostensibly to reclaim his former love, Kate. He has significantly been transformed by his overseas experience and is unrecognized by friends and former neighbors, except for Kate. He proves to be the catalyst that permits others to fulfill their dreams, even if he cannot bring to life his own dream, marriage to Kate, for she has married Michael.

The young family is in financial trouble, and so the generous and loyal Christy arranges to lose the fifty pounds they need, a very considerable sum of money in those days, to Michael in a game of cards called Twenty-Five. Then he departs for America once more, leaving from a community dance, where in farewell to Kate he says: "You wouldn't refuse the greatest stranger in the house. Give me a dance now and I'll be thinking of you sometime when I'm dancing with some high up lady, having golden shoes, in a white marble court by the sea." He leaves with a gallant flourish: a kiss for Kate and a wave of his hat for the neighbors.

Lady Gregory's dialect Irish English is similar to but not as metaphorical or lyrical as Synge's. Her play, however, is six years older than *The Playboy of the Western World,* and surely it paved the way for the ultimate acceptance of Synge's creative diction if not his plot and character constructs. The Kiltartan dialect of Lady Gregory's country people is never used for disingenuous sentimentality, and there are no stage Irishmen in her work.

The Rising of the Moon (1903)

The Rising of the Moon is not a comedy, but rather a very short, thrilling one-act play about an Irish rebel escaping from the police. It does have light moments, however. Set on a quay in a seaside town at midnight, the play opens with three policemen looking for a rebel and thinking about the hundred pounds reward for his capture. A ballad singer attempts to frighten off the sergeant of the police by warning him that the fugitive has killed. They sit together, keeping watch, and the singer entertains the policeman with song and implants the thought that he should attempt to change places in his mind with the rebel. When a boat approaches for the fugitive, a song, "The Rising of the Moon," a rebel song, is heard as the signal for the escape attempt. In the end, the sergeant, now sympathetic, helps the fugitive to get away.

Spreading the News (1904)

Recognized as Lady Gregory's little comic masterpiece, *Spreading the News* is her most performed and most anthologized play. The play is based on a misunderstanding that results in a rumor that is embellished as it passes from person to person. No one intends to delude anyone else, but massive misinformation runs rampant, the village people being eager to gossip.

At a country fair, Bartley Fallon tries to return a hay fork to his neighbor Jack Smith, who had accidentally left it at the apple stall of Mrs. Tarpey, a woman quite hard of hearing whose misinterpretations cause much of the play's mischief. Bartley's wife says that he has gone after Smith with a hayfork—meaning, of course, that he wants to return it. Mrs. Tarpey then hears that Mrs. Smith is laying out a sheet on a hedge but believes that she has heard "laying out a sheet for the dead." Now people assume that Bartley and Mrs. Smith are having an affair and that he wants to do in Smith. A policeman and a magistrate are called in, and Bartley is placed under arrest, handcuffed, and charged with murder. His wife berates him, and Smith does the same, believing the rumors of the affair. Blunders are amplified. The magistrate, ostensibly an Englishman, is led to believe by misunderstanding the constable that murders frequently occur at the fair. The magistrate often remarks that he has a system for law enforcement: "When I was in the Andaman Isles my system never failed." Of course, he is not in the Andaman Isles, but in the "United" Kingdom of Great Britain and Ireland. To English civil servants, however, one colony is just like another; natives are natives.

Lady Gregory must surely be gently satirizing her deceased husband, that long-serving colonial administrator. In the end, Smith is also arrested because he is accused of impersonating the deceased Smith! He desperately wants to kill Bartley. Poor innocent, well-meaning Bartley, realizing that he may shortly prove to be the corpse, says: "It is what I am thinking, if myself and Jack Smith are put together in the one cell for the night, the handcuffs will be taken off him, and his hands will be free, and murder will be done that time surely!"

In *Spreading the News*, the Irish people at the fair say and do funny things, but they are not disrespected or ridiculed by the author. Here in Lady Gregory's work, as in Synge's, dislike of police is significantly a common underlying assumption about rural Ireland. Although the play is a comedy, with suspense, surprise, and farcical actions, its characters and situations are still plausible, not absurd, and the audience is left with a feeling of affection for the people of the country fair, a feeling shared with the author. Mild ridicule and satire are directed at the magistrate and the not too bright policeman, Joe Muldoon, who has bought into the English occupation and distanced himself from the other village people.

Hyacinth Halvey (1906)

A darker and more complex play than *Spreading the News*, *Hyacinth Halvey* is the story of a young man, an assistant sanitary inspector, who comes from Carrow to live in Coon. Because he has come so highly recommended, he has no privacy and lives under the parish priest's constant scrutiny. Furthermore, he is required to perform some difficult and unpleasant duties because he is such a role model. He must wear a teetotaler's button and give morally uplifting lectures to farmers.

Halvey wants fun and his former freedom of action, so he attempts to extricate himself from the restrictive character his letters of recommendation have created. He tries to steal a sheep but fails to do evil because he inadvertently saves the butcher, whose tainted meat was to be confiscated. (It is sometimes hard to be bad if one has not had much practice at it.) Then he and his inept accomplice, a messenger boy, attempt to rob a church, but only the boy is accused. Halvey, determined to ruin his reputation, confesses to the crime, but the community considers him to be a heroic martyr and even more saintly. The cheering crowd and the system—church and state—have him in their stifling embrace forever. He *will* be respectable. The community is all powerful. The witty play has some of Lady Gregory's most well-crafted dialogue. Coon springs to life as if the playwright were creating portraiture.

The Jackdaw (1907)

Set in a general store in Coon, *The Jackdaw*, like *The Playboy of the Western World*, indicates the somewhat condescending belief of Anglo-Irish writers such as Lady Gregory and Synge that Irish peasants need a hero to worship even if they must construct that person from false information, half-lies, and gossip. Nevertheless, *The Jackdaw* is one of Lady Gregory's funniest and most popular plays.

The general store owner is Mrs. Broderick, a middle-aged, illiterate widow in debt and nearly bankrupt. She hopes that her well-off brother, Cooney, a farmer near Limerick, will help her, and she has her friend, Joseph Nestor, write letters to him. There are no answers, and the poor woman must go to court. Cooney comes to town and tells Nestor that he wants to help his sister but doesn't want her to know that he is the source of her relief for fear that she will become dependent on him. Cooney is no generous unselfish hero like Christy in *Twenty-Five*.

Lady Gregory seems to be answering her heroic portrait of Christy with that of the pragmatic, loss-cutting Cooney, whose name seems to symbolize the people of the area. Nestor fabricates a wild yarn about an Irish-born South African mine owner who is lonely for Ireland and wants the company of an Irish bird that is able to survive in a dark mine. Only one bird fits the bill: the jackdaw, a bird that lives in chimneys. The owner supposedly has sent ten pounds through an agent to pay for one. Mrs. Broderick is given Cooney's much-needed money for her pet jackdaw. But Cooney, too, believes Nestor's concocted story and goes off to an old mill looking for more jackdaws to sell.

Unwilling to tell people how she got the ten pounds, Mrs. Broderick sees her reputation in the community slipping and attacks Cooney for not finding a bird to deliver to the imaginary agent. Meanwhile, everyone in the village from the magistrate on down goes on a bird hunt looking for jackdaws to sell to the "agent." Although Mrs. Broderick is informed that the money came from Cooney, she refuses to believe it and is unsatisfied: "Satisfied is it? It would be a queer thing indeed I to be satisfied. My brother to be spending money on birds, and his sister with a summons on her head." At the end of the play, the fatuous police force is searching for the missing "agent," the principals are afraid they will be arrested for a nonexistent crime, and the audience is left laughing at the unending farce.

Nestor, named after the wise old Greek, has been made a local hero solely because he is a learned man and can spin a good yarn. He is more like the merrygreek of early Renaissance English comedy, bent on clever mischief, a character itself derived from the wily slave of Roman comedy. Nestor does not deserve any adulation, of course, and so the play gently satirizes the gullibility of the West Country folk.

The Gaol Gate (1908)

A very short curtain-raiser tragedy, *The Gaol Gate* shows West Country peasant hatred for British law and the informers who kept the system going. In the play, two women visit a jail where a man—son and husband—is held as an informer. Upon arrival, they are told that the man has died. They are sad that he will have the bad name of an informer. When they are given his clothes and told that he was hanged, it is good news for them, and they rejoice because he would not have been hanged if he had informed. Their kin is not a traitor after all; he gave his life for Ireland. Lady Gregory is preaching the individual's self-sacrifice for the sake of the oppressed community. She had become a literary rebel herself.

The Workhouse Ward (1908)

Originally called *The Poorhouse* and based on Lady Gregory's knowledge of the workhouse in Gort, *The Workhouse Ward* satirizes Irish pretentiousness and absurd pride, as evidenced in two sickly, old, indigent men, ancient antagonists and once feuding neighbors who now continue the feud from adjoining beds. Each one claims a finer lineage and higher status than the other. When the sister of one of the men arrives with a suit of clothes to take him out of the workhouse, he refuses to go without his old enemy, to whom he is sentimentally attached. The sister wants only one man—as cheap labor—not two, and so she starts to leave with the suit, but the old men speed her departure by pelting her with everything they can lay their hands on. Lady Gregory saw in the Irish character a great need for community and a deep-seated craving for talk. Indeed, it's better to have someone to argue with than to be alone.

The Full Moon (1910)

In *The Full Moon*, Lady Gregory, as if to draw her comedies into a folk circle, employs a host of characters from earlier plays, such as Bartley Fallon from *Spreading the News*, Mrs. Broderick from *The Jackdaw*, Hyacinth Halvey, and others.

Halvey supposedly has been bitten by a mad dog, "as big as a calf . . . a milch cow. . . . Terrible wicked he is; he's as big as five dogs, and he does be very strong." (The animal, in fact, is small, tame, and safe.) The people of Coon believe the rumor and, afraid that they will be bitten by Halvey, attempt to chain him up, just as the Mayo people in *The Playboy of the Western World* tied up Christy Mahon, the seemingly mad-dog parricide near the end of the play. In the end, Halvey escapes, realizing that he does not have to live among the "insane" people of Coon, the sanest of whom is Cracked Mary, the former resident of the local madhouse.

The Bogie Man (1912)

A well-constructed two-character play, *The Bogie Man* is set at a coach stop, where two impoverished chimney sweeps meet. Neither is happy to run into "one of my own trade," so each one boasts to the other about his affluent first cousin, a paragon of virtue and a most competent and able youth—in other words, an impossible role model. Each is boasting to appear to be of a higher social position than the other. As the boys change their clothes and wash the chimney black off their faces, they recognize each other. They are the cousins. They good-naturedly assert that they will never weave untrue fantasies again to make themselves more important than they are. Moreover, they are going to be pals. The audience enjoys both the early moment of recognition when it first realizes that each of the lads must be the cousin awaited by the other and the second moment of recognition later when the characters learn the same.

Darner's Gold (1912)

Lady Gregory's miser play is indebted to Molière's *L'Avarice* (The Miser), which in turn is based on Platus's *Aulularia* (The Pot of Gold). Darner, a miser, has a gallon jug nearly full of gold coins that is his pride and joy. Darner's brother, his niece Delia, and her husband enter Darner's home and discuss his miserliness while he, in hiding, eavesdrops on them. He refuses any attempt by them to make his home more livable because it would require spending money.

In act two, the miser changes, becomes generous and charitable, and begins to enjoy life. His relatives, especially Delia, think he has gone mad and plan how to spend his money. But Darner has lost his money playing cards with a man named Simon, who turns out to be a nephew in disguise. The other relatives are frustrated as the former miser and his pleasure-loving nephew, now strongly bonded, go off to enjoy the money. Like Molière, Lady Gregory applauds generosity and those who take pleasure in life. As a wealthy aristocrat who was also a generous person, Lady Gregory felt she was in a position to chastise the greedy Delias of the villages and countryside.

Hanrahan's Oath (1917)

A slight comedy, *Hanrahan's Oath* is about a garrulous poet, Hanrahan, whose name is taken from Yeats's stories in *The Celtic Twilight* and who is possibly based on Yeats. Hanrahan believes that because he talks too much, he has informed on a friend who has kept an illegal still. He vows an oath of silence, and people think he is a holy man until he learns that his friend has not been convicted, at which point he becomes garrulous again.

A widow, Mary Gillis, a rooming-house owner with whom Hanrahan has been lodging, may be a humorous self-portrait of Lady Gregory. Mary Gillis tries to trick Hanrahan into staying with her, but the poet leaves her with a curse as he goes off with a young woman named Margaret Rooney. In the same year that this play was produced, Yeats married a very young and affluent Englishwoman, Miss Bertha Georgie Hyde-Lees, and seemed to be about to desert Ireland for life in England. *Hanrahan's Oath* may have been Lady Gregory's way of dealing with what she thought was the loss of a dear friend. Fortunately, the friendship endured for the rest of her life.

Additional Reading

Gregory, Lady Isabella Augusta. *Our Irish Theatre.* 1913. Reprint. Gerrards Cross, U.K.: Colin Smythe, 1972.

————. *Selected Plays of Lady Gregory.* Washington, D.C.: Catholic Univ. of America Press, 1983.

Kohfeldt, Mary Lou. *Lady Gregory: The Woman behind the Irish Renaissance.* New York: Atheneum, 1985.

Saddlemyer, Anne. *In Defence of Lady Gregory, Playwright.* Dublin: Dolmen, 1966.

Tóibin, Colm. *Lady Gregory's Toothbrush.* Madison: University of Wisconsin Press, 2002.

WILLIAM BUTLER YEATS (1865–1939)

William Butler Yeats was Ireland's greatest poet and arguably the leading poet of the English language in the twentieth century. Yeats became as large a legend as any ancient hero or bard he sang about. In his lifetime of genius and creativity, his poetry continued to mutate, develop, extend, and grow in profundity and power. As *the* poet of the new Irish nation, he made Ireland and things Irish culturally fashionable in the marketplace of the English-speaking world.

In addition, Yeats was the prime mover of and major spokesperson for the Irish Literary Revival; he was an essayist, an autobiographer, a mystic, an Irish senator, an ardent opponent of censorship and proponent of free artistic expression, the 1923 recipient of the

Nobel Prize for Literature, and, of course, a founder of the Irish National Theatre Society.

Yeats, the author of two dozen plays, always thought of himself primarily as a dramatist. Indeed, he was a playwright of importance, and as a founder and codirector of the Abbey and its predecessor for more than half of his lifetime, he helped make Dublin for the first twenty-five or thirty years of the twentieth century a theater capital, its productions equal in originality, profundity, and creativity to those in any city in Europe or the Americas. He made a contribution to Irish and European culture that remains a source of great pleasure and pride in Ireland, and his work was and still is a foundation for much outstanding literary achievement in Ireland.

Yeats's creative life had two great psychological secrets. First, he was a counterrevolutionary, intellectually and emotionally battling his father, who was himself in revolt against the values of the Victorian age. Second, he was always mindful of the fact that he was the son of the Irish bourgeoisie, clergy and businesspeople, not of the landed gentry, and he aspired to be accepted by or even to become one of the latter.

Born in Dublin, William was the eldest of four surviving children in a talented Protestant family headed by the fine portrait painter, raconteur, and impractical husband-father John Butler Yeats and the quiet, sensitive, Sligo-reared, Sligo-loving, ever-worrying mother Susan Pollexfen. "Willy" spent his early childhood in Sligo, while John Butler Yeats, previously trained as a lawyer at Trinity College, Dublin, studied painting in London. Yeats's siblings also grew up to be artists. His brother, Jack B. Yeats, became one of Ireland's most renowned painters.

Young William was taken from beautiful Sligo to London along with the rest of the family so that they all could live together again with their father. Yeats studied at the Godolphin School in Hammersmith. When the Yeats family moved back to Dublin in 1880, William attended the High School, Harcourt Street. His father wanted his firstborn son to attend Trinity College, Dublin, as he had, but Yeats, a poor student, never could have passed the entrance exam, and so he chose the Metropolitan School of Art and then the Royal Hibernian Academy. There he became a lifelong friend of George Russell, the poet AE, and Russell introduced him to fellow mystics, beginning Yeats's fascination with the occult.

It must be pointed out that Yeats's childhood, adolescence, and early manhood years were lived against the defeats and retreat of his class, the Protestant middle class, and of the class he admired, the Protestant Anglo-Irish Ascendancy. The Land War and the land acts weakened the landowners' control in jumps and starts. Home Rule—if not full independence—seemed to be coming. Surely these events that his father supported (but the rest of his family did not) helped turn Yeats's thought and then his art toward the romantic and safely dead Irish past.

In 1886, Yeats decided on a writing career instead of one in the fine arts, and he began producing poetry based on English models and without Irish content. Then, under the influence of the old Fenian fighter John O'Leary, Yeats turned to Irish subjects and themes.

The Yeats family went back to London in 1887. There Yeats met Madam Blavatsky and joined the Theosophists and the Order of the Golden Dawn. Yeats would later state that the mystical life was central "to all that I think and all that I write." In 1891, Yeats was one of the founders of the Rhymers' Club in London. He also became active in the literary politics of Irish writers in London, founding the Irish Literary Society of London in 1891 and, with other people, the National Literary Society in 1892, an organization to promulgate the literature, mythology, legends, and folklore of Ireland. Yeats's contribution to the movement, also his first literary success, was his long mythological poem *The Wanderings of Oisín* (1889). Four years later another major publication, *The Celtic Twilight,* showed his growing skill in prose and his ability to turn folklore into readable material for the contemporary public.

In 1889, Yeats met the great love of his life, the beautiful Maud Gonne. His painful, unrequited love for her would be a source of inspiration and intense pain for him for much of his life because Maud Gonne refused him again and again. Gonne made Yeats into a Republican, and under her influence he joined the Irish Republican Brotherhood and began to be more active politically.

According to her diary, Lady Gregory and Yeats first met in the spring of 1894, the same year that his first stage production, *The Land of Heart's Desire*, played in London. The wealthy, aristocratic woman became his most important friend, and their mutual influence was of incalculable significance to them and to Irish culture. Spending many summers at Coole Park with Lady Gregory, Yeats found the calm, security, and natural beauty he needed in order to write some of his finest lyrics and plays.

As noted earlier, the idea of an Irish theater came into existence in September 1897, at the end of the very first summer Yeats spent at Coole, when Yeats and Lady Gregory met with her neighbor Edward Martyn of Tulira Castle at Duras House, County Galway. The next year the three founded the Irish Literary Theatre, forerunner of the Irish National Theatre Society, whose playhouse was known as the Abbey. In 1899, Yeats's first play to be produced in Ireland, *The Countess Cathleen*, starring Florence Farr, was performed in Dublin. The second, *Diarmuid and Grania* (1901), was a failed collaboration with the novelist George Moore.

Earlier, in 1896, while still residing in London, Yeats had visited Paris and met John Millington Synge. Their friendship endured for the rest of Synge's short life. Yeats urged Synge to stop trying to be a French symbolist writer and return to Ireland to study peasant life and search Irish roots for subject, theme, and language. Synge did, to the glory of Irish drama.

In 1902, Yeats returned to Ireland and became president of the Irish National Theatre Society. His *Cathleen ni Houlihan,* secretly coauthored by Lady Augusta Gregory, starred Maud Gonne that year. The famous play was considered politically inflammatory, but it survived censorship. It remains Yeats's most often performed drama. The next year Yeats made the first of several lecture tours of the United States, where he was greeted with great acclaim. In 1903, his poetry collection *In the Seven Woods* appeared.

At the Abbey's first performance in 1904, Yeats's *On Baile's Strand,* one of his finest plays and the first of five dramas based on the legend of the epic hero Cuchulain, was on the bill. The next year *The King's Threshold* was performed. *Poems 1899–1905* was published in 1906, the same year that Yeats's *Deirdre* was first performed at the Abbey. Two years later Ezra Pound met Yeats, becoming an ardent admirer and even his secretary for a short period. Pound introduced Yeats to Japanese Noh drama and thus influenced his later playwriting because Yeats found himself fascinated with the Noh's use of masks, symbols, and ritual dancing. Yeats continued to write poetry and plays prolifically, publishing *The Green Helmet and Other Poems* in 1910, the same year his name appeared on the British Civil List for an annual pension of 150 pounds per annum.

In England in 1911, Yeats met his future wife, nineteen-year-old Bertha Georgie Hyde-Lees, later affectionately known as "George." They would keep in touch and then marry six years later. When his friend and protégé Synge died in 1909, Yeats edited the younger writer's *Poems and Translations* as a memorial act of friendship and homage.

In 1903, Maud Gonne had married Major John MacBride, who had fought the British in the Boer War. The marriage was not a happy one. But MacBride was, like Gonne, an Irish patriot, and he was one of the leaders of the 1916 Easter Rising, for which he, along with other leaders, was executed by the British government. Yeats, a supporter of the failed rebellion, wrote several poems in honor of the martyrs.

But Yeats's mind was also on founding a family, belated though the thought was. Thus, he purchased a decrepit medieval Norman tower near Coole, County Galway, a site he had first seen when walking with Lady Gregory years earlier. His plan was to marry and bring his bride to Thoor Ballylee; he would renovate the tower, creating a summer home environment for the family and a place in which he could communicate with the spirits of the past and the stars in the night heavens. Maud Gonne turned him down again, and the following year, smitten by her daughter Iseult, he proposed marriage to her, but she too rejected Yeats. George, now twenty-five, was next on the fifty-two-year-old Yeats's list, and she said yes. A daughter, Anne Butler Yeats, was born in 1919, and a son, William Michael Yeats, in 1921.

Meanwhile, the poetry collection *Responsibilities* appeared in 1914, the play *At the Hawk's Well* was produced in London in 1916, *The Wild Swans at Coole* was published in 1917, and *Michael Robartes and the Dancer* was published in 1920. With the Anglo-Irish War and then the Irish Civil War raging, Yeats, who supported the treaty establishing the Irish Free State and opposed the IRA's rebellion against the new Irish government, spent more time in England than in Ireland, either in Dublin or Ballylee, for the safety of his family. He finally established a central Dublin residence, 82 Merrion Square, in 1922, the year he became a member of the Irish Senate and just prior to the world recognition that came with the Nobel Prize for Literature the next year. In 1922, *Four Plays for Dancers* appeared in print.

Yeats adapted Sophocles' *Oedipus Rex,* and the play was performed at the Abbey in 1926. Still considered the outstanding poetic and dramatically playable translation of the ancient Greek classic, his adaptation is frequently read as a school text. It was brilliantly performed by the Canadian Shakespeare Festival at Stratford, Ontario, in a production directed by the festival founder Tyrone Guthrie and presented with masks. Yeats's adaptation of Sophocles' *Oedipus at Colonus* (1934) has proved less popular.

Also in 1926, Yeats helped to design the new Irish coinage, creating beautiful modernist animal designs on the obverse sides of the coins—no heads of presidents or heroes for him. Alas, the current euro coinage is a much less attractive, artless successor. In 1928, he published a memorable poetry collection inspired by Thoor Ballylee, *The Tower.*

In the last decade of his life, Yeats moved between London, Dublin, and Ballylee and Coole Park in Galway. In 1932, the year his dear friend Augusta Gregory died, the Yeatses moved from Merrion Square to Riversdale in Rathfarnham, County Dublin. Riversdale was his final residence in the country of his birth.

With George Bernard Shaw and AE, Yeats founded the Irish Academy of Letters in 1932. *The Winding Stair and Other Poems* appeared in 1933, along with *Collected Poems; Collected Plays* appeared in 1934; and a Salomé play, *A Full Moon in March,* was published in 1935. Yeats's creativity, especially in poetry, continued throughout his life.

In the meantime, Yeats also worked on his autobiography (which does not tell the reader much about his actual life) in installments: *Reveries over Childhood and Youth* (1915), *The Trembling of the Veil* (1922), and *Dramatis Personae* (1936).

With his health failing, Yeats went to warm his ailing body on the French Riviera in the winter of 1938. Visits to the South of France in winters past had been beneficial; on this trip, though, he died—at Roquebrune, near Monaco, on 28 January 1939. He was temporarily buried there, but World War II prevented the return of his body to Ireland until 1948, when an Irish warship brought his remains home to Ireland. After ceremonies in Dublin, his body was taken to his beloved Sligo, and he was buried in Drumcliffe churchyard, next to the parish church that had once been his grandfather's. Yeats had always wanted to be buried in sight of the great Sligo mountain, "under bare Ben Bulben's head." He had written his instructions for an epitaph:

No marble, no conventional phrase;
On limestone quarried near the spot
By his command these words are cut:
>Cast a cold eye
>On life, on death
>Horseman, pass by!

These words were so cut on limestone. But Yeats had not cast a cold eye on life. His time here had been warm, full, and graced with love, friendship, respect, and the power to move both people and, indeed, a nation.

George devoted much of the rest of her life to the task of being the family archivist. She died in 1968.

Plays

William Butler Yeats was a passionate man who used passionate language. He saw in drama the possibility of depicting the irreconcilable, irresolvable conflicts of life. He believed in the greatness of the human spirit and soul—a greatness that was best manifested by noble action under tragic situations. To him, human greatness was a symbol on earth of God's greatness.

Yeats always attempted to concoct a unique brew of symbol and scene, sound and sense, ritual and reality, and action and thought. Myths and archetypes, those mind capsules of eternal truths, were the primary means by which Yeats communicated his passion and intensity to his audience. Although a mythomane, Yeats also wrote peasant plays (with the help of Lady Gregory), but his heart was with those of his characters based on folk legends and Irish mythology. Looking at the totality of his dramatic work, one quickly realizes that he was an innovator, an experimentalist, and a ritualist in style and dramaturgy. His favorite themes were those that emphasized heroic action and noble sacrifice. He knew as well as anyone that romantic Ireland was dead and gone, but his commitment to lyricism and his love of beauty put him at odds with Ibsenites determined to show the poverty and sordidness of rural and urban contemporary Irish life. To Yeats, Ireland was a beautiful queen, not the old, grasping, bigoted hag whom other writers, the realists and naturalists, sometimes saw.

For Yeats, writing drama was something of a priestly occupation, and the theater was a sacred place of mystery and patriotism. Not surprisingly, he referred to some of his dramas as mystery or morality plays. And Yeats learned from Sophocles and Shakespeare that inner conflict reflects conflict in God's universe, while humans suffer and weep for order. In his drama, he reached for that divinity that is within humankind, finding it in heroes and heroines who move, like Plato's shadows, as the prototypes of our spiritual world. Thus, for Yeats, character is destiny, and destiny is within character.

The Cuchulain Saga

Between 1903 and the last week of his life, Yeats wrote five plays on the life, exploits, and death of his favorite epic hero from the Ulster Cycles, Cuchulain: *On Baile's Strand* (1904), *The Green Helmet* (1910), *At the Hawk's Well* (1916), *The Only Jealousy of Emer* (written 1919, performed 1922), and *The Death of Cuchulain* (1939). One might surmise that Yeats was most proud of his one epic dramatic cycle.

On Baile's Strand (1904)

Yeats wrote *On Baile's Strand* as if he were an Irish Sophocles. His hero is brought to his fall by the flaws of his character, pride and rashness, as well as by his fate. His final struggle, a mad battle with the sea, is perhaps Yeats's adaptation of that quixotic courage in the Irish character that led to so many glorious defeats in Irish history at the hands of overwhelming invaders.

The heroic warrior Cuchulain, the man of passion and action, at first opposes the clever, crafty high king Conchubar, but the king is skilled at manipulation, and finally the hero submits, takes an oath, and as a pledge must kill in combat a certain brave young man. His intuition tries to restrain him. He wants to befriend the young man, but to no avail. The king forces the combat, and Cuchulain slays the youth, who turns out to be his own son, the product of a brief, youthful affair with the warrior queen Aoife—a son of whose existence he was unaware. The intelligent but passionless and heartless Conchubar has orchestrated everything in order to preserve the succession of his own sons. Cuchulain cannot fathom or accept his tragic fate. He has no son to carry on his name; just as he believed would be his fate before he knew of his son's life and caused that son's death, he will be remembered only by the harp. Thus, in madness he marches into the army of waves, striking them with his sword as he is overwhelmed by the sea.

Like Greek tragedy, *On Baile's Strand* is written in verse and employs a chorus of women for intensification and heroic speeches from the oral tradition for the rituals of historical identification and confrontation. A thieving blind man and a singing fool, both in masks, symbolize the king's craftiness and the hero's passionate love of life, respectively. The play is a superb wedding of symbol, archetype, and action—a work of great aesthetic beauty.

The Green Helmet (1910)

The lightest of Yeats's Cuchulain dramas, *The Green Helmet*, has comedy as well as dramatic suspense, and the hero is presented at his most magnanimous, committed to the joie de vivre. His generous and noble conduct is meant to contrast with the meanness Yeats saw in his contemporary Ireland. The play is structured around three episodes, each employing the same characters, but each also having its own denouement. At the beginning of the play, the presence of the Green Helmet agitates the warriors. Three warriors fight over the right to wear the Green Helmet, a possession and an action denoting precedence, and Cuchulain resolves the conflict by filling the helmet with ale and having the warriors drink the same amount, thus symbolizing their equality and friendship. Then he flings the trouble-causing helm into the sea.

In the second episode, each of three great ladies, all wives of heroes, wishes to enter the banqueting hall first because each believes her husband is the greatest hero and she therefore deserves primacy of place among the wives. Like Solomon or Odysseus, wise Cuchulain solves the dilemma by not letting his own wife, Emer, enter before the other two women have broken passages in the wall so that all parties may enter simultaneously. Face is saved, and vanity served.

Finally, Cuchulain offers himself as a pledge for the honor of his people when the supernatural Red Man comes to take Cuchulain's life. Instead, however, the Red Man presents Cuchulain with the Green Helmet symbolic of Cuchulain's championship. Cuchulain is the greatest of the heroes, ready to defend his right to the honor of being the champion.

The satire on the human frailties and vanities of the heroes and their wives is quite amusing, and it gives the play a realism and earthiness that the other Cuchulain dramas do not contain.

At the Hawk's Well (1916)

One of Yeats's most beautiful plays, *At the Hawk's Well* explores the possibilities of the Japanese Noh dramatic tradition employed in the service of Irish legend. This powerful, energy-filled drama uses masks, drum, gong, zither, highly stylized dancing that is simultaneously modern and ancient, an especially significant and aesthetically satisfying chorus, and some of Yeats's finest dramatic imagery.

Although *At the Hawk's Well* was the third Cuchulain play written by Yeats, it precedes all the others in the order of the epic. Here the young, headstrong, confident Cuchulain is initiated into his role as signifier of a culture and a history. He comes to the Hawk's Well to drink from the magical water so that he may become godlike— immortal, passionate, and creative—but there he is confronted by the guardian of the well, a crafty supernatural woman who tricks him from his purpose by luring him into the woods to seduce him, but then she disappears.

Cuchulain, unable to couple with the immortal, must satisfy himself with living flesh. This feeling is appropriate and natural for a youth of his age, for the young must always choose the pleasure and the purpose of the temporal world. Unbeknownst to him, his sexual encounter with Aoife sets the stage for the most tragic episode in his saga, for she is to be the vengeful mother of the son he will slay one day. Although Cuchulain is defeated in his attempt to capture the waters of immortality, he exults in the realization that his destiny is to live: to thrive not in the supernatural world, but in the world of human passion, desire, and frailty. Cuchulain's character contrasts with that of the old man who has lived by the well for fifty years and who is satisfied with the most meager portion of life. Cuchulain intuitively understands that the length of one's life is not what is significant; it is the passion and range of a life's experience that marks its value.

The Only Jealousy of Emer (written 1919, performed 1922)

The Only Jealousy of Emer is one of the group Yeats titled Four Plays for Dancers. They are written in the Noh style with music and highly ritualistic and symbolic movement by dancers. In The Only Jealousy of Emer, Cuchulain is a shadowy, dreaming figure who recalls the past with remorse. The play begins with a melancholy lyric about the frailty and the glory of a woman's beauty. Next, in a fisherman's cottage, Cuchulain lies in a trance. He has been brought from the strand and is near death. His wife, Emer, summons his mistress,

Eithne, to his bedside to attempt to return him to life, a deed that Emer is unable to accomplish.

The Only Jealousy of Emer is a verse play about marriage and the ancient triangle of lust and jealousy: husband, wife, husband's lover. Cuchulain dreams on, and then Eithne woos him back to the land of the living. Masks are used to present the many, complex sides of character. Cuchulain's darker faces drive the mistress from his side, but the wife must see all sides of the husband, even his low, unreachable ghost-spirit. Yet—above all—Emer wishes to regain her husband's love, but she heroically is willing to forego that love forever if doing so will bring back the old spirit of the hero she loves. She moves beyond jealousy to sacrifice. He will awake, but never in her arms. The married couple communicate on the deepest level with few words, but with the feeling and understanding that comes from long, familiar love.

The Death of Cuchulain (1939)

The dying Yeats and the dying Cuchulain finally merge in Yeats's last play—or, at the least, Yeats "signs" his epic plays by having one character, an old man, refer to "the old epics and Mr. Yeats' plays about them."

As Cuchulain moves toward death, his wife, the wise Emer, attempts to prevent the old hero from battling the offspring of the witch Calatin because Emer knows that the old hero is unable to defeat their power of enchantment, but Calatin's one-eyed daughter, Badh, provokes him. Another daughter, the Moorage, Irish goddess of war, attempts to prevent the hero from engaging in the battle by damaging his war chariot, but to no avail. Cuchulain will not be detained. In the fierce battle, he is mortally wounded, leaves the field to find water, ties himself to a standing stone, and is killed and beheaded by the blind man of *On Baile's Strand*. The plays are linked. Emer mourns, and the warrior Conall takes revenge. Yeats has rounded up all the old cast of the Cuchulain cycle in *The Death of Cuchulain*—Queen Maeve, Emer, the vengeful Aoife, the mistress Eithne, and others—for the grand finale, and with it the Cycle of Cuchulain is over. Was the hero's "life" of passionate action the life Yeats himself had longed for?

Other Mythic Plays

The Shadowy Waters (1904)

Forgael the poet-harpist-hero abducts Dectora from her husband, King Iollan, who is killed. Dectora attempts to command her abductor and his men, but Forgael prevents her from doing so. Forgael is transformed or reborn as her rightful husband and king, and they are joined in immortal love. Forgael stands for human intellect and reason, and Dectora represents sexuality. The story is a human one raised to the divine by sublime poetry.

Deirdre (1906)

Despite the fact that the tragedy *Deirdre* is based on the world-renowned story of the love of Deirdre and Naoise, the Irish equivalent to the tale of Tristan and Iseult, it is not successful. Yeats had not yet assimilated the values and the power of Sophoclean tragedy. It is Synge who brings dramatic passion and life to this great love story in his *Deirdre of the Sorrows*. Nevertheless, the character of Deirdre is beautifully portrayed by Yeats. Again a warrior king—this time Conchubar—loses the love and the possession of his young bride to a younger man. The king is the old crafty bourgeois. Naoise is the brave man of action. In the ensuing battle, Naoise is made prisoner and ignominiously executed. Youth is once more denied its natural triumph. Deirdre cannot live without young love. With her concealed knife, she takes her own life to join her lover in death.

Political Plays

Cathleen ni Houlihan (with Lady Augusta Gregory) (1902)
Yeats's most famous and most frequently performed play, *Cathleen ni Houlihan* is one of those works of art that influence history. Long after the first performance and after young men had died in the Easter 1916 attempt to free Ireland from British rule, Yeats considered what he had wrought: "Did that play of mine send out / Certain young men the English shot?" ("The Man and the Echo"). The words are famous; the question more than rhetorical. Yeats and other early dramatists did inspire the patriotism that first led to failure and then to success.

The play is set in a cottage in the West in 1798, the fateful year of a failed Irish revolt, and the story begins when a poor, old peasant woman, Cathleen ni Houlihan, who symbolizes Ireland, convinces Michael Gillane to leave his fiancée and his comfortable life to join other Irish people and the invading French to fight the English for the nation's freedom. He rushes from his lover's arms and dashes out at Cathleen's call. The last words of the play are spoken by Michael's father ("Did you see an old woman going down the path?") and his son Patrick ("I did not, but I saw a young girl, and she had the walk of a queen"). Ireland can be transformed from poor peasant to beautiful queen only by the dedication and brave sacrifices of her young.

The Dreaming of the Bones (1931, first published 1919)
A dance play based on Noh dramaturgy and style, *The Dreaming of the Bones* presents a confrontation between the ghosts of the past, Diarmuid and Dervorgilla, who were the royal pair responsible for bringing the Norman Conquest and English rule to Ireland in the twelfth century, and a young Irish revolutionary who fought with Ireland's heroes at the post office during the Easter Rising of 1916. Diarmuid and Dervorgilla are tortured by the knowledge that they

betrayed their race. Only forgiveness from one of their race can end their agony, but the young man cannot find it in his heart to do so. He can forgive almost anyone, but not these traitors. The play ends with Diarmuid and Dervorgilla performing a Dantean dance of penance and remorse.

Purgatory (1938)

Another ghost story, *Purgatory* is a Greek-like tale of the need to purify a family from the sin that cursed it. At the ruins of Castle Dargan near Sligo, an old man, a peddler of the West, informs his son of the history of the derelict house. Ghosts of the house appear. The boy and the father fight over a paltry sum of money, and the boy is slain with the knife his father had used against the boy's grandfather.

These mean men represent the Irish of Yeats's present, and the castle stands for his ruined nation, split and tortured by continual dissension and division. The murder replicates past manifestations of the curse, and the play ends with the old man praying that God will let the dead be still and end the sufferings of the living. But it is only after the passion has burned out that purgatory may be escaped. Compact, sparse, and tight, the play succeeds on both the level of political allegory and the level of generational tragedy.

Folk and Fairy-Tale Plays

The Countess Cathleen (1899)

Yeats revised *The Countess Cathleen* again and again—in 1901, 1912, and 1919—and made minor changes from time to time. Clearly, he saw in the character of the countess a personification of the noble Irish nation—someone who would do anything, make any sacrifice, for the people.

Opposing the attempts of two demon merchants to buy the souls of the starving peasants, the countess sells her own soul to them to save her people. (Although the poet Kevin tries to sell his soul to prevent Cathleen from selling hers, his effort is in vain.) However, because the countess is pure and saintly, her soul does not go to hell, but instead to heaven, where it is welcomed with great joy as the play ends. Through self-sacrifice, she has defeated the forces of evil. Subsequent versions of the play are more complex, but the initial, simpler text seems to work best.

The Pot of Broth (1902)

This play, so reminiscent of Lady Gregory's subjects and style, is one of Yeats's very few comedies. Using simple and direct dialect language, the short play has a nameless tramp as hero—actually antihero because he lives by his wits and his words as he cadges for his daily bread. He shows a "magic" stone to an avaricious woman, Sibey Coneely, and gets her to put food into the pot with the stew-providing stone. The foolish woman is saved from further duping only by the imminent arrival of the parish priest and thus the quick retreat of the clever tramp. *The Pot of Broth* says yes to the freedom of the road and the triumph of wit over the bourgeois values of those with fixed abodes and materialistic vision. The plot is related to the Russian folktale "Stone Soup."

The Hour-Glass (1903, 1914)

Yeats chose to rewrite this play extensively ten years after its first production—changing the dialogue, converting prose to verse, and adding some of the experimental staging he had embraced in his career as a dramatist. It is the rewritten version with masks that is usually studied and occasionally performed. *The Hour-Glass* is a morality play and allegory like *Everyman*. The Wise Man finds salvation through humbling himself to the Fool, Teigue. An angel causes him to change his arrogant ways. Yeats wants the skeptical intelligentsia of his time to accept the possibility of miracles. The "fools" of the world are the holy people who believe—who are connected to the reality of the spiritual. The road to salvation for the "wise" is to accept God's will completely.

The King's Threshold (1903)

Yeats evidences his concern for the role of the poet and artist in society in *The King's Threshold*. He also advances the concept of the ideal hero-citizen: a combination of sensitive poet and person of action. The society that neglects the artist's role is tragically handicapped. Seanchan, the passionate bard, is also a man of action. His antagonist, the king, is a political creature, a man of reason, and a materialist.

A general conspiracy exists to corrupt Seanchan and to deprive him of his idealism. Church, state, and army work on him. Though tempted by flattery, love, beauty, and sex, he does not succumb. The poet-hero goes to his death (by hunger strike) undaunted and safe in his convictions, an example for all.

Additional Reading

Ellman, Richard. *Yeats: The Man and His Masks*. New York: Macmillan, 1948.

Foster, Roy. *W. B. Yeats. A Life*. Vol. 1: *The Apprentice Age*. London: Oxford Univ. Press, 1997.

———. *W. B. Yeats. A Life*. Vol. 2: *The Arch-Poet*. London: Oxford Univ. Press, 2003.

Taylor, Richard. *A Reader's Guide to the Plays of W. B. Yeats*. New York: St. Martin's Press, 1984.

Unterecker, John. *A Reader's Guide to William Butler Yeats*. New York: Noonday, 1959; Syracuse, N.Y.: Syracuse Univ. Press, 1996.

Yeats, William Butler. *The Collected Plays of W. B. Yeats*. New York: Macmillan, 1953.

———. *Eleven Plays of William Butler Yeats*. Edited by Norman A. Jeffares. New York: Macmillan, 1964.

GEORGE BERNARD SHAW (1856–1950)

Like his fellow Dublin-born playwright Oscar Wilde (1854–1900), George Bernard Shaw had a distinctly Irish wit but made his contribution to the drama and the theater in England. He is represented relatively briefly here because of only one major play about Ireland, the controversial *John Bull's Other Island* (the very title could raise a Republican's temperature ten degrees).

Shaw was born into the Protestant lower middle class, the one son and third child of George Carr Shaw, a heavy-drinking, continually failing merchant, and Elizabeth Gurly Shaw, a woman who had pretentions to a career as a singer. Her music teacher, George Vandeleur Lee, moved into the house on Upper Synge Street (33 Synge Street) and formed the third leg of a marital triangle. Shaw received a secondary education at Wesley College but could not attend Trinity College, Dublin, because of lack of funds. What amounted to his higher education came in part through music that he heard at home and in part from many hours of reading and his study of pictures in the National Gallery. At sixteen, he was a clerk in a business office. When the music teacher left for London, Mrs. Shaw followed.

Shaw was left with his father for four years, and then in 1876 he joined his mother and her lover in London, where she supported her son while he wrote one unsuccessful novel after another. Shaw did not return to Ireland for nearly thirty years. For nine years of literary effort, he earned almost nothing. Moved by the plight of London's poor, he joined the Fabian Society and became an effective speaker for socialism. Finally, Shaw obtained employment as a music critic. William Archer, the drama critic and theorist, found him additional work as a book and theater reviewer.

In 1892, Shaw turned to playwriting with his attack on slumlords, *Widowers' Houses*. Other plays then followed, including *Mrs. Warren's Profession, Arms and the Man,* and *Candida,* but his first major success was *The Devil's Disciple,* and thereafter came *Man and Superman, Major Barbara,* and the ever-popular *Pygmalion.* In 1898, Shaw married an affluent Anglo-Irish woman, Charlotte Payne-Townshend. Joining with the producer-playwright Harley Granville-Barker at the Royal Court Theatre, Shaw soon became Britain's leading playwright.

At Yeats's request, Shaw wrote *John Bull's Other Island* for the Irish Literary Theatre in 1904, but the play was not shown in Dublin until much later. In London, it was an instant success. During World War I, Shaw was an ardent and vociferous pacifist, and for that he was blackballed and nearly imprisoned. Fame returned after the war with such plays as *Heartbreak House* and *St. Joan;* he received the Nobel Prize for Literature in 1925. The Shaws had no children. Charlotte Shaw died in 1943, and Shaw continued writing up to his death in 1950.

Shaw was an Ibsenite. He took Henrik Ibsen's concept of the thesis play—in which a problem of society is presented for consideration by the society itself, as represented by the middle-class audience—and employed it in social comedies that sparkled with wit and wonderful dialogue. Without doubt, Shaw was the greatest playwright of the English language since Shakespeare. His only possible challenger is that very different master of existentialist drama, Samuel Beckett, who is discussed later.

Plays

John Bull's Other Island (1904)

In typical Shavian fashion, *John Bull's Other Ireland* inverts the expected cliché: the play's chief and typical Englishman, Tom Broadbent, is the sentimentalist, gushing over monastic ruins and the peasant life, whereas the play's chief Irishman, Larry Doyle, is a hard-headed realist, critical of Irish values and self-delusion, without sentiment for Irish ways or Irish women. Although Broadbent is sentimental about old Ireland, he is a clever businessperson who makes a substantial profit from Ireland, marries the girl who has been waiting years for the indecisive Doyle, and actually gets to represent an Irish constituency in the British Parliament because the Irish people would rather be represented by a wealthy, free-wheeling, malarkey-spreading Briton than one of their own. Shaw thus satirizes the English middle-class professional who seems such a role model for the Irish and the middle-class Irishman who makes his living in England and who out of admiration has become more English than the English.

The plot of the play centers on the conquest of an Irish village, Rosscullen, by Tom Broadbent, an English engineer and land developer. This conquest is a symbolic microcosm of the relationship between England and Ireland as Shaw saw it at the turn of the twentieth century and as many Irish people still see it today—thus the continued interest in the play. Broadbent's Irish partner, Larry Doyle, whose original home is Rosscullen, should be the one leading his community into the opportunities of the new century, but he is too indecisive, too cynical, and too skeptical about the abilities of his fellow Irish to commit himself, assume the leadership that is needed, and even marry the Irish girl, Nora, who loves him and has been waiting for him. The ever-optimistic Englishman and his countrymen will thus inherit Ireland by default and grow even more wealthy by capitalist exploitation.

The spokesperson for socialism who has a program for a utopian state is an unfrocked Catholic priest, Peter Keegan. But he is an eccentric visionary who sometimes talks to grasshoppers. He is a St. Francis. But he does not have the political authority to alter the inevitable results of the English affection for and obsession with John Bull's other island.

Some of Shaw's funniest characters and most challenging, thought-provoking dialogue grace this great Irishman's "plague o' both your houses!" Today Shaw's views on Home Rule are of interest primarily to historians, but his delightfully satiric representations of the conflicting Irish and English characters and of the mixed-message, postcolonial colonialism of a wealthier, ever-patronizing Britain toward its small neighbor and that neighbor's seemingly quixotic population are astoundingly relevant still.

In 1905, a year after *John Bull's Other Island* opened in London, King Edward VII ordered a royal command performance; convulsed with laughter, the portly monarch of Great Britain and Ireland broke his chair and fell to the floor. In the end, the Irish had the last laugh.

Additional Reading

Gordon, David J. *Bernard Shaw and the Comic Sublime.* New York: St. Martin's Press, 1990.

Holroyd, Michael. *Bernard Shaw.* New York: Random House, 1993.

Shaw, George Bernard. *George Bernard Shaw's Collected Plays with Their Prefaces.* Edited by Dan H. Laurence. New York: Dodd, Mead, 1970–74.

Smith, Warren Sylvester. *Bishop of Everywhere: Bernard Shaw and the Life Force.* University Park: Pennsylvania State Univ. Press, 1982.

JOHN MILLINGTON SYNGE (1871–1909)

More than any other Irish dramatist, John Millington Synge captured the harsh truths, the painful lives, the soothing and necessary blind faith, the poetry of the oral tradition, and the humor of the poor folk of Ireland's West. Synge was the first truly world-class Irish dramatist of the modern age who worked in the Irish theater, and *The Playboy of the Western World,* his comic masterpiece and the glory of early-twentieth-century Irish drama, is the most frequently performed and read Irish play of the early period.

Edmund John Millington Synge was born of Protestant stock in Rathfarnham, County Dublin, to a lawyer and Galway landowner, John Hatch Synge, who died a year after his son was born, and

Kathleen Traill Synge, a daughter of an evangelical Ulster Protestant clergyman. John, the youngest of five children, grew up and spent much of his life among women—mother, grandmother, and sister—which explains the strong older women in his plays. After his early private education, he attended Trinity College, Dublin, and the Royal Irish Academy of Music simultaneously, becoming an academy orchestra violinist determined to pursue a career as a professional musician. At this phase of his life, he rejected his inherited formal religion to become an individualistic lover of nature, a mystic, and an aesthete.

In pursuit of advanced musical training, Synge journeyed to Germany in 1893, where he suddenly decided on a writer's career. He therefore moved to Paris, then the center of European culture and literature. On vacations, he visited Ireland's west coast and made his first trip out to the Aran Islands. Back in Paris, he met Yeats, who advised him to return to Ireland, especially to the Aran Islands, to find his subjects, narratives, and language.

From 1899 to 1902, Synge was a regular and accepted summer visitor on the islands, listening, observing, and taking notes on the ancient and isolated life of the fisherfolk. Synge's first book, *The Aran Islands,* illustrated by Yeats's talented brother, Jack B. Yeats, was later published in 1907. Meanwhile, Synge began to write plays for the new Irish National Theatre. Synge's two great one-act plays, *In the Shadow of the Glen* (1903) and *Riders to the Sea* (1904), were his brilliant first efforts in a genre completely new to him.

After the opening of the Abbey Theatre in 1904, Synge became one of its directors, and *The Well of the Saints* was first produced there the next year. In 1907, *The Playboy of the Western World* provoked a riot at its Abbey opening, nationalists objecting to its portrayal of the Irish character and others objecting to the mention of a woman's undergarment in public. *The Tinker's Wedding* was written in 1902 and published in 1908. It was not produced by the Abbey in Synge's lifetime because of its anticlerical scenes.

Synge died at thirty-eight of Hodgkin's disease on 24 March 1909, before completing his last play, *Deirdre of the Sorrows*. His work was already a success in London, and the Abbey company would soon take it to America for more riots and everlasting fame. The early international recognition of modern Irish drama as a major contributor to world theater and literature rested on the handful of plays Synge left behind. A generation later O'Casey renewed and enhanced that recognition.

Plays

Synge's plays, in spite of comic elements, are melancholy works. The heroes are sweet-talking men who try to take the women of their choice from staid domestic worlds into the adventure of life. The performance of his plays, so full of truth they hurt, were always events. And in time these plays became part of the national life of Ireland.

The Shadow of the Glen (1904)

Although Synge first heard the story on Inishmaan in the Aran Islands, he chose to set his play in a County Wicklow glen near his home, Glenmalure. The story of a jealous old man pretending to be dead in order to test the fidelity of his young wife, however, is an ancient one, as is the tale of the eternal triangle of the old husband, the young wife, and a young lover. Both have been used for tragedy and comedy, and both contribute to Synge's plot. Nora Burke's old husband, Dan, is distasteful to her. For her, the marriage was based on her desire to have some security in her life. In the pattern of Irish marriages of the past, Dan, "with a bit of a farm with cows on it, and sheep on the back hills," had waited until late in life to marry a young, strong, and desirable woman.

Tricked into believing that the husband is dead, Nora and her young lover, Michael Dara, plan to take Dan's money and marry, although she worries that life with Michael might be a repeat of life with old Dan. Michael is concerned primarily with the money. Then Dan "rises from the dead" and orders Nora out of his house.

The cowardly, parsimonious Michael will not go out into the world with the penniless woman. Instead, she departs with a tramp, a symbol of freedom, who promises her song, sun, and a good companion in bed. The husband and the lover, instead of falling to blows, are content in the end to drink to each other's health in whiskey, the water of life. The play is a tragicomedy, much more Irish than Greek, for in the end the vital woman seems superfluous as the contending farmers end up happy and sociable in their new friendship and their drink.

Riders to the Sea (1904)

The only play of Synge's set in the Aran Islands, *Riders to the Sea* is the playwright's darkest, most tragic drama. The presence of irre-vocable fate is so strong in the play—and it so engrossed Synge's creative sensibilities—that for the first and only time in his dramas language recedes, and plot takes center stage.

Central to the drama is the character of Maurya, one of the first archetypal, all-suffering, all-sacrificing Irish mothers in mod-ern Irish drama. She has given her husband and one son to the sea, and now she must watch helplessly as yet another son, Bartley, her last, wills himself to ride his horses to the sea and the eternity that the sea symbolizes. Maurya must tell the story, just as she must do her duty to provide clothing for the living and coffins for the dead and to keen them. Men, cut off in their prime, continually enter the cemetery of the waves, as Maurya reminds us: "There does be a power of young men floating round in the sea."

Bartley dies, almost perversely, not as a fisherman, but as a wild young man who is determined to take his animals to the horse fair on the mainland and in consequence has a riding accident at the shore. But the fateful sea will claim its catch as it can. The tragedy of *Riders to the Sea* is the most ancient of all, the greatest grief: the death of the young before the old.

The Well of the Saints (1905)

Synge drew on his knowledge of French literature in writing *The Well of the Saints,* based in part on a French morality play of the fifteenth century. His two blind, indigent protagonists, Martin and Mary Doul, surely inspired Beckett's creation of more than one beggarly pair (as in *Endgame* and *Waiting for Godot*). In morality plays, names of characters are significant and help in characterization. The word *doul* is Irish for "blind," and this blind pair are happy despite their affliction. They rant, rave, and abuse each other, but they live contentedly in their own world, and this world is a rich, variegated, and beautiful one because it exists in their colorful imaginations. Each believes, for example, that the other is very attractive, although in fact both are far from it.

The saint at the well miraculously restores their sight. Although at first they are delighted, each soon comes to realize the other's and then his or her own ugliness and how unpleasant looking and acting the world and the sighted are. They no longer have a great deal to say to each other. Their worlds are now individually different, and each one seems too large.

Now they must toil for a living, pitifully paid as road workers. They separate for a while, but as their sight dims again, they rediscover each other and reunite in their happy relationship. Realizing that they have been misused by the controlling holy man, they spurn the saint, his asceticism, and his miracles. Although the blind couple are driven out onto the road by the villagers, a higher place is clearly waiting for them. It is the palace of self-knowledge, reason, sensuality, and confidence, as evidenced by Mary's curtain line: "The Lord protect us from the Saints of God."

The Playboy of the Western World (1907)

Synge succeeded in his stated goal for *The Playboy of the Western World* to write in "English that is perfectly Irish in essence." The language, the broad characterizations, the humor, the precise structure, and the satire of the play are so excellent that without doubt the work is not only a masterpiece, but the greatest single play ever to have been written in Ireland.

The play's setting is a country public house in Mayo. Although its publican is Michael Flaherty, his daughter, Pegeen, does most of the work and runs the establishment. She is betrothed to Shawn Keogh, an unattractive, cowardly, priest-ridden cousin for whom neither she nor the audience has much respect.

When a pitiful fugitive, Christy Mahon, comes into the house and announces that he has murdered his father, a farmer like himself, the unprepossessing young man becomes an instant hero to Pegeen and the community. Even an older woman, the wily Widow Quin, sets her cap for him. But Christy cares for Pegeen, and she is in love with the young "hero," who conjectures: "Wasn't I the foolish fellow not to kill my father in the years gone by?"

After preening himself and milking the situation, the now-cocky Christy finds his story finally unraveling when his father appears, head slightly dented, but very much alive. Christy, who actually believed he had killed his father, now has lost face, and so he "kills" his father again. But this time the community is aghast; as Pegeen says, "there's a great gap between a gallous story and a dirty deed," and she even burns Christy to break his hold on a table. But tough Old Mahon is still not "killed." He reappears, this time full of admiration for his son because, in confronting his father, Christy has proved his manhood.

Christy now disdains Pegeen and the community and marches off, his father following respectfully. The young hero has, in the tradition of comedy, overcome the impediment of the older generation's power. But poor Pegeen utters the lament of many a young

Irish woman: "Oh, my grief, I've lost him surely. I've lost th playboy of the Western World."

The Playboy of the Western World is the finest Irish comedy just as *The Importance of Being Earnest* is the finest English comedy. Of course, both were written by Irishmen. And both plays are ultimately about language: the profound incongruity between the poetry and wit of a delightfully crafted story and the realities of life that words distort or incompletely signify.

The Tinker's Wedding (written 1902, significantly revised for publication 1908)

Because of this play's anticlerical thrust and a scene in which a grasping parish priest is gagged and tied up for his willingness to let a couple go without the sacrament of marriage unless they meet his material demands, the Abbey did not put on *The Tinker's Wedding* until 1971. The Rabelaisian comedy pits Michael Byrne, a crafty tinker—that is, a person of the roads (now called a "traveler") who lives like a Gypsy but is not actually one—against a priest who wants to extract as much money and goods for his services as he can. The tinker's companion, Sarah Casey, craves middle-class respectability and thus wishes to be married. Michael reluctantly agrees to have his relationship with his woman sanctified by marriage because, like a bourgeois, he has patriarchal economic reasons for tying up his woman as wife: "If I didn't marry her, she'd be off walking to Jaunting Jim maybe at the fall of night, and . . . there isn't the like of her for getting money and selling songs to the men."

He wants to keep possession of her sexual favors and her earning ability. The priest is reluctantly willing to marry the couple for the seemingly bargain price of half a sovereign, but he also wants a can (drinking vessel) that the tinker (traditionally a pot mender and tinsmith) is making. Michael tries to trick the priest out of the can, but the priest then refuses to marry the couple and orders them off. The tinkers tie him up and gag him with the sack that had held the can, and then, in an ending like a Ben Jonson comedy, the couple run for their lives. Of course, Michael and Sarah will continue to live in sin, although they pledge their troth to each other in a "tinker's wedding."

The play feels and sounds like a medieval folk play. Farce provides much of the humor, and rich characterization makes *The Tinker's Wedding* a play that has grown in popularity as an alternative to the more often produced *Playboy* and *The Well of the Saints*.

Deirdre of the Sorrows (1910)

Completed by Yeats and Lady Gregory, the tragedy *Deirdre of the Sorrows* was premiered by the Abbey in the year after Synge's death. The signature Synge language enriches the play, and it is certainly warmer and more feeling than Yeats's *Deirdre,* but in the end the story remains more fitted for the romantic poem of earlier versions than for a workable drama.

The play is passionate. Deirdre and Naisi's love is erotic and ecstatic. The Celtic past is presented in soft-focus nostalgia. Yet the plot line is timeless and international: the dark and deadly triangle of an old man, his young bride, and her young lover. Conchubor, the cuckolded king, is like a darker Arthur; his jealousy-inspired treachery in luring the heroine, the hero, and the hero's two brothers back to Ireland from Scotland—resulting in the three men's death and Deirdre's suicide—is terrible but humanly understandable.

Young love cut off is paradoxically both mortal and immortal. But the consequences of adultery and revenge are catastrophic: a palace in flames and a kingdom on the verge of destruction. Synge gives the persuasive Deirdre, who almost convinces her husband to spare her lover, a great last speech, echoing that of Shakespeare's Cleopatra. It includes lines that are as true for Synge as for any mythic hero or heroine: "I have put away sorrow like a shoe that is worn out and muddy, for it is I have had a life that will be envied by great companies."

Additional Reading

Gerstenberger, Donna Lorine. *John Millington Synge*. Boston: Twayne, 1990.

Greene, David H., and Edward M. Stephens. *J. M. Synge 1871–1909*. New York: Macmillan, 1959.

Grene, Nicholas. *Synge: A Critical Study of the Plays*. London: Macmillan, 1975.

Kiberd, Declan. *Synge and the Irish Language*. London: Macmillan, 1979.

Kiely, David M. *John Millington Synge: A Biography*. New York: St. Martin's Press, 1995.

King, Mary C. *The Drama of J. M. Synge*. Syracuse, N.Y.: Syracuse Univ. Press, 1985.

Synge, John Millington. *J. M. Synge: Complete Works*. London: Oxford Univ. Press, 1968.

7

Other Early-Modern Dramatists

OF COURSE, other playwrights besides Lady Gregory, Yeats, Shaw, and Synge contributed to the growth, development, and success of the Irish drama before O'Casey. Outstanding among these dramatists were Padraic Colum, T. C. Murray, George Fitzmaurice, Lennox Robinson, and George Shiels. Of these early writers, Padraic Colum was the one who seemed most destined for greatness and perhaps literary immortality.

PADRAIC COLUM (1881–1972)

Padraic Colum liked to say that of all the Irish playwrights of his time, he was the only one who was Roman Catholic and peasant born. He also liked to say that he was born in the workhouse of Longford, which was technically true, but his father was master there. Colum's mother was the daughter of a gardener. With a minimal education, Colum followed his father to Sandycove, County Dublin, to work as a railway clerk. Beginning to write poems and one-act plays, he came to the attention of Arthur Griffith, editor of *The United Irishman* and later the first president of the Irish Free State. Colum linked up with the Abbey as both playwright and actor. The three full-length plays he wrote between 1903 and 1910—*Broken Soil* (1903; revised and retitled *The Fiddler's House* for the 1907 revival), *The Land* (1905), and *Thomas*

Muskerry (1910)—established him briefly as the Abbey's most popular playwright.

The brash young writer, who also had great initial success as a lyric poet with his first collection of poems, *The Wild Earth* (1907), quarreled with Yeats and the Abbey company, and despite Lady Gregory's attempt to effect a reconciliation, he quit the company. In 1914, he left for America with his wife, Mary McGuire Colum, who in New York became one of America's leading critics in the early twentieth century. Colum had no success as a playwright in New York, try as he would, but he continued to publish well-received and still revered volumes of poetry, folklore, and children's books until his death in Connecticut just before his ninety-first birthday. One of his most popular nondramatic books is *Our Friend James Joyce* (1958), which he coauthored with his wife.

Plays

The Fiddler's House (first titled Broken Soil, 1903; revised and revived, 1907)

Conn Hourican is a middle-aged peasant farmer who has to choose between the romantic life of an itinerant musician and his obligation to his children and the land. The allegorical play pits Conn, the freedom-loving artist, against James Moynihan, the grasping son of a miserly father. Conn chooses the road, and his loving daughter, Maire, goes with him, but her lover, Brian, woos her back. The play's strength is its authentic depiction of peasant characters.

The Land (1905)

Produced at the Abbey on 9 June 1905, just six months after the theater opened, *The Land* was the new theater's first popular success—to some extent because it is about the Land War, which had fairly recently been concluded, and the passage of the Land Purchase Act, which allowed peasant farmers for the first time the opportunity to purchase and own the land on which they and their families had worked for centuries.

Two elderly farmers, Murtagh Cosgar and Martin Douras, try to keep their four children on the land by arranging two marriages between them. In the end, however, the bright couple leave to immigrate to America, and the good-hearted but dull couple remain to inherit the land. Colum is saying that, for many, land ownership came too late, and the best of the young were and are leaving. The lamented emigration of talented youth has remained a vital theme in Irish drama to the present.

Thomas Muskerry (1910)

Based on Colum's recollection of life in the Longford workhouse his father administered, *Thomas Muskerry* is his only pure tragedy. It resembles *King Lear* in its portrayal of a workhouse master who in his retirement and old age is treated cruelly by his daughter, who in turn is mistreated by her daughter. Colum is showing how hardheartedness is passed on from generation to generation as well as how frail and fleeting human dignity is.

Additional Reading

Colum, Padraic. *Selected Plays.* Edited by Sanford Sternlicht. Syracuse, N.Y.: Syracuse Univ. Press, 1986.
———. *Three Plays.* Dublin: Maunsel, 1917.
Sternlicht, Sanford. *Padraic Colum.* Boston: Twayne, 1985.

T. C. MURRAY (1873–1959)

Thomas Cornelius Murray was born in Macroom, County Cork. He trained as a primary school teacher at St. Patrick's Teachers' Training College in Drumcondra, and education remained his primary work until he retired in 1932.

Murray was a playwright who invested almost his entire stock in dramatic realism; his best plays offer a grim and often tragic portrait of Irish peasant life. He also strove to show the religion of the peasant, Irish Catholicism, in a kinder light than other early-modern Irish dramatists. *Maurice Harte* (1912) and *Autumn Fire* (1924) today are considered his finest dramas.

Plays

Maurice Harte (1912)

Combining Ibsen-like social drama and the peasant scene much in the manner of Padraic Colum's *Thomas Muskerry* (1910), *Maurice Harte* is the story of devoted parents who have sacrificed almost everything to educate a son for the priesthood, only to find that the son has lost his vocation for the life of a priest. The father and mother, Michael and Ellen Harte, entreat their son, Maurice, to return to the priesthood for their sakes. Moved by his mother's pleas, Michael miserably decides to go back, but in the end he has a nervous breakdown from the stress, and his parents, especially his mother, are filled with guilt. The convincing dialogue and the powerful characterization are the primary strengths of this play about religious struggle.

Autumn Fire (1924)

An elderly widower, Owen Keegan, proud of his good health and physical prowess, marries a woman thirty years his junior. The community disapproves. His daughter, Ellen, is angered, and his son, Michael, evidences his own interest in the bride, Nance. Owen soon suffers a stroke, and Michael grows closer to Nance, so Ellen informs on them and makes her father jealous. Though Michael must leave home, and the invalid father cannot believe in his wife's innocence, the blighted marriage goes on. The archetypal story is as current today as it was in the Athens of Euripides and early-twentieth-century Ireland.

Additional Reading

Connolly, Terrence L. "T. C. Murray, the Quiet Man." *The Catholic World* 190 (March 1960): 364–69.
DeGiacomo, Albert J. *T. C. Murray, Dramatist: Voice of Rural Ireland.* Syracuse, N.Y.: Syracuse Univ. Press, 2003.
Murray, T. C. *Autumn Fire.* London: Allen and Unwin, 1928.
———. *Maurice Harte.* Dublin: Maunsel, 1912.

GEORGE FITZMAURICE (1877–1963)

Born the son of a Protestant minister who had crossed the line to marry a Roman Catholic girl, Fitzmaurice grew up between cultures and eventually seemed to fall in the crack. He spent most of his youth with his mother's peasant Catholic family, but he was gentry by birth because his paternal relatives were Ascendancy.

Fitzmaurice's life was to a large extent that of a recluse. He moved to Dublin in 1901, and his first play at the Abbey was *The Country Dressmaker,* presented in 1907. The comedy remained a favorite play for Abbey audiences for some forty years. He served in the British army in World War I and became a civil servant to earn his living, working for the Department of Agriculture until retirement. He died in an impecunious state.

George Fitzmaurice followed close on the heels of Synge and Colum with his peasant plays. The typical locale in his plays is a peasant cottage. Although Fitzmaurice's themes, like Colum's, are marriage, emigration, and the lust for land, he differs from Colum in his use of the fantastical and the whimsical. Almost all of his seventeen plays are set in the world of his childhood, the northern region of County Kerry, and he attempts to replicate the local dialect in his dramas.

Plays

The Pie-Dish (1908)

In *The Pie-Dish*, a one-act fantasy, Fitzmaurice employs his characteristic technique of mixing realistic situations with the fantastical and supernatural. It is the story of a dying old man, Leum Donoghue, who desperately fears that he will not be able to complete an ornamental dish on which he has been working for twenty years. To buy more time, he offers his soul to the devil. The tricky devil accepts. But when Donoghue finishes the dish, it falls from his hands and shatters just as he drops dead. It's the old Faustian bargain, of course, but the audience loved the play's irony and Irish setting.

The Magic Glasses (1913)

The one-act play *The Magic Glasses* is set in Padden and Maineen Shanahan's kitchen. Jaymony Shanahan, their thirty-eight-year-old son, spends his time in a loft looking through nine lenses purchased from a fairy. Through them, he sees a better world, a fantastic place. A conflict results when his desire to merge with his fantasy world causes him to behave strangely, alarming his family.

Believing Jaymony mad, they call in a charlatan miracle worker, Mr. Quille, to cure him. Quille blasphemously "exorcises" Jaymony, prescribes a ridiculous regimen, and departs, but the devil seems to have possessed the family, for the loft collapses, Jaymony falls to his death, and the other inhabitants rush out of the house, screaming in terror. A madness that should have been only humorous and harmless has ended in catastrophe and death; the audience, like witnesses to a morality play in the Middle Ages, is stunned by the powerful, frightening, melodramatic denouement.

Additional Reading

Fitzmaurice, George. *The Plays of George Fitzmaurice.* 3 vols. Dublin: Dolmen, 1967, 1969, 1970.

Gelderman, Carol W. *George Fitzmaurice.* Boston: Twayne, 1979.

McGuinness, Arthur E. *George Fitzmaurice.* Lewisburg, Pa.: Bucknell Univ. Press, 1975.

LENNOX ROBINSON (1886–1958)

Best known as the Abbey manager and then director, Lennox Robinson was also a playwright, novelist, essayist, theater historian, and author of a two-volume autobiography. His well-made plays feature middle-class, small-town Irish life.

Esme Stuart Lennox Robinson, the son of a Protestant clergyman, was born in Douglas, County Cork, and was educated at Bandon Grammar School. He saw the Abbey company performing on tour in Cork in 1907 and fell in love with the theater. On and off and in various posts, Robinson served the Abbey as an administrator from 1909 to his death in 1958. His first Abbey play was *The Clancy Name* (1908). His best-known plays are the comedy *The Whiteheaded Boy* (1916) and the Chekhovian drama *The Big House* (1926). Much honored at the end of his life, Robinson is buried in St. Patrick's Cathedral, Dublin.

Plays

The Whiteheaded Boy (1916)
The working-class comedy *The Whiteheaded Boy* depicts how some younger sons wind up in no-win situations. Denis Georghegan's older siblings scrimp and save and sacrifice their own futures to send him to a university so that he can receive a medical degree. But Denis does not want to be a doctor, nor does he have a particular

aptitude for medicine. The siblings have not sacrificed cheerfully, but somewhat grumpily, and when Denis leaves to become a laborer, one expects them to be glad to have the expense no longer. However, they now join forces to prevent such a disgrace to the family. The story and its ironies are engaging.

The Big House (1926)

Given the current nostalgia for the Irish country mansion and its Ascendancy inhabitants as well as the popularity of Brian Friel's play about an Irish Big House, *The Aristocrats* (1979), there should have been a revival of *The Big House* by now. When Robinson wrote the play, it seemed that none of the great houses would survive; nearly two hundred of them had been destroyed between 1921 and 1923, the period of the last months of the Anglo-Irish War and the post-treaty Irish Civil War. *The Big House* presents the dilemma of a well-meaning, socially responsible Ascendancy landlord family, the Alcocks, as they are trapped in a struggle based on political and class differences. The house referred to in the title is Ballydonal House in County Cork, where the Alcock family learns on Armistice Day, 11 November 1918, that the second and last son, like his brother before him, has been killed in action in France. Then the house, very much a character in the play, is threatened with destruction by Irish guerrillas during the Anglo-Irish War as retaliation when the Black and Tans, British rampaging auxiliary police, are randomly killing. But it is spared because of the village people's loyalty to and respect for its inhabitants. But later in the Civil War, Ballydonal is burned by Republicans, and the family breaks up. The father and mother retire to England, but the sensitive daughter, Kate, realizes that, regardless of class or religion, she is Irish, not English. Thus, she plans to rebuild, continuing to make her lonely life in the country of her birth as it is being reconstituted as an independent state.

As in Anton Chekhov's *The Cherry Orchard*, in *The Big House* a family is caught up in forces far beyond its control; but in this play, unlike in Chekhov's, a tradition and a rebuilt estate will live on and contribute to the new era. *The Big House* is a moving play of historical significance and a fine piece of theater. Kate Alcock is one of the best-drawn women in the early-modern Irish school of realism.

Additional Reading

Murray, Christopher, ed. *Selected Plays of Lennox Robinson*. Washington, D.C.: Catholic Univ. of America Press, 1982.
O'Neill, Michael J. *Lennox Robinson*. New York: Twayne, 1964.

GEORGE SHIELS (1886–1949)

Born in Ballymoney, County Antrim, George Shiels immigrated to Canada in 1906 but returned to Antrim seven years later after suffering crippling injuries in a train accident. He took up writing without any formal instruction in the craft. He, like George Fitzmaurice, was quiet and reclusive; although he was a very popular dramatist, he hardly ever left his home in Carnlough, even to see one of his own plays performed.

Between the two world wars, George Shiels gave Ireland snapshots of itself in realistic, gently satirical comedies and dramas based on the new country's need for equal justice and for law and order. His playwriting career began with two one-act plays performed at the Ulster Literary Theatre in Belfast: *Under the Moss* (1918) and *Felix Reid and Bob* (1919). His first plays for the Abbey, *Bedmates* and *Insurance Money*, both also one-act plays, were produced in 1921. His first major successes were *Paul Twyning* (1922) and *Professor Tim* (1925). With these works, Shiels established his own brand of rural Ulster kitchen comedy, complete with cleverly subdued social commentary. *The Passing Day* (1936) is his strongest, most satirical, and bitterest play. In 1940, *The Rugged Path* broke Abbey Theatre records, playing to twenty-five thousand people in eight weeks. In the period after O'Casey, Shiels was the mainstay of the Abbey Theatre. All in all, he wrote twenty-three plays, including full-length ones as well as one-acters. *Professor Tim* was made into a Hollywood film.

Plays

Paul Twyning (1922)

The title character is an itinerant laborer who enjoys mischief making. A skillful liar who convinces people of his truthfulness, he sets about to disrupt a family, turning members against each other. James Deegan, a magistrate of the Crown, a person new to money and middle-class status, is his chief victim. Love and lovers play a part in the comedy. Paul turns suitors against each other, but in the convention of romantic comedy the right men win the predestined brides, and even Paul winds up with a lover.

Professor Tim (1925)

In *Professor Tim,* a romantic comedy that takes place in a single day, a young man named Hugh O'Cahan is in financial difficulties and about to lose Peggy Scally, the girl he loves and who loves him. Her mother insists that she marry a wealthy suitor, but, of course, true love wins out in the end.

The Passing Day (1936)

Set in six scenes that take place in one day, *The Passing Day* is the story of three mean characters living in a small town filled with an unsavory population. John Fibbs, a wealthy merchant and town leader, is a sly, miserly, hard old man. His wife, Sarah, is a resentful puritan. His nephew, Peter, adopted as their only child, pretends, like Edmund in *King Lear,* to be an obedient son, but he really would like to murder his hated uncle. (Peter himself is incapable of loving anyone, even his devoted girlfriend.) At the beginning of the play, Fibbs is on his deathbed in the hospital. In the course of the play, all who try to extract money or advantage from Fibbs are exposed: wife, doctor, lawyer, nephew, acquaintances. *The Passing Day* is much like Ben Jonson's *Volpone*—as biting, if not as funny.

Additional Reading

Kennedy, David. "George Shiels: A Playwright at Work." *Threshold* 25 (Summer 1974): 50–78.

Sheils, George. *The Passing Day and The Jailbird*. London: Macmillan, 1937.

———. *Three Plays: Professor Tim, Paul Twyning, The New Gossoon*. London: Macmillan, 1945.

8

The Sean O'Casey Era and After

AFTER SYNGE, the next truly world-renowned dramatist to arise from the Irish theater was Sean O'Casey. His three tragicomedies, *The Shadow of a Gunman* (1923), *Juno and the Paycock* (1924), and *The Plough and the Stars* (1926), are centered on the then recent events of the War of Independence and the Civil War and are set in the Dublin slums that O'Casey knew so well. They turned the Irish theater for a while toward bitter social criticism: O'Casey's dark thesis was that the acclaimed and glorified birth of a nation was accompanied by the pathetic suffering, powerlessness, and tragedy of the unknown and little-regarded common people swept up and drowned in the raging, mindless torrent of history.

O'Casey was a self-taught playwright. He came to his art by seeing some plays in Dublin, but mostly by reading playwrights such as Ibsen, Strindberg, Shakespeare, and the other Elizabethans. He also read the plays of the most popular Irish dramatist of the nineteenth century, Dion Boucicault, from whom he learned much about dramatic structure.

O'Casey is the playwright of the disintegrating community and of the fragile family that in the end has only love (but can't even count on that). O'Casey's ear for the dialect of the Dublin tenements is very sharp. He had heard enough of it. Like Synge, he shaped and lyricized dialogue, adding dignity to the utterances of the poor.

After the Dublin trilogy, O'Casey, having written out of his system much of his cynicism and skepticism regarding Irish government, patriotism, religion, and politics, became more and more an experimental dramatist, but *The Shadow of a Gunman, Juno and the Paycock,* and *The Plough and the Stars* stand as monuments that rose unexpectedly in the very shadow of the Abbey—and out of the pain of a compassionate person who shared with many others the disillusionment with life and society's institutions that came when the heady achievement of independence, alas, did not lead to promised peace or work or food.

Born John Casey, Sean was the youngest of five surviving children in a lower-middle-class Dublin Protestant family that sank to working-class status after the death of the father—a clerk for the Irish Church (Protestant) Mission—when O'Casey was three. The family moved often, each time to less-comfortable quarters. Crowded Dublin was a very unhealthy place for adults as well as for children in the late nineteenth century. It is difficult to know the full details of O'Casey's childhood because the writer tended to mythologize it. Clearly, his mother Susan O'Casey did all she could to maintain a degree of respectability for the family. Sean was sickly, malnourished, and troubled with life-long vision problems caused by trachoma, which prevented him from obtaining more than a cursory elementary education. His sister Isabella, a schoolmistress, provided most of his early education, teaching her younger brother to read.

O'Casey found employment as a laborer. At night, he pursued his religious and political interests: his local church; the Orange Lodge for Protestant men; the Gaelic League, which he joined in 1906 and where he studied Irish (and Gaelicized his name to "Sean O'Cathasaigh"); the Irish Republican Brotherhood; and the Irish Citizens Army, the political and militant arm of the Irish Transport and General Workers' Union. One by one, however, these organizations disappointed him, and, disgruntled, he shed them all.

He resigned from the Irish Citizens Army when the organization backed Patrick Pearse's call for revolt, and O'Casey criticized the fateful Easter Rising of 1916.

At this time, O'Casey began writing journalism, history, poetry, and even greeting-card verses for a Dublin publisher. He eventually came to dramatic writing after realizing when he was in his forties that he could use his lifetime of observing Dublin tenement life to provide authentic dialogue. The venue for his dramatic ambitions, the Abbey Theatre, was within easy walking distance. By 1920, he was writing plays. Another name change followed, and now he was Sean O'Casey.

In 1923, O'Casey, after four rejections, offered a two-act play, *On the Run*, to the Abbey. Lady Gregory at last was enthusiastic. The play was put on at the season's end as *The Shadow of a Gunman*. O'Casey had given tenement life in Dublin, which other writers had treated with little success, its first fully effective dramatic portrayal. *Juno and the Paycock* and *The Plough and the Stars* quickly followed. The latter, however, was greeted with hostility by the audience and brought riots once more in and around the Abbey because an Irish writer seemed to be ridiculing Irish patriotism and nationalism as well as the Irish character. Yeats's reaction was a speech to the audience in which, alluding to the riots over *The Playboy of the Western World*, he said, "You have disgraced yourselves again!"

Hurt, O'Casey took the play to London, where he had received the Hawthornden Prize for *Juno and the Paycock*. In London, he married an Irish singer-actress, Eileen Carey, who performed in West End productions of his plays. O'Casey's next play, experimental and expensive to mount, was a drama about World War I, *The Silver Tassie*, written in 1928. To his surprise and chagrin, the Abbey rejected it. Yeats was ungracious and ungenerous this time. He didn't like modernist dramas and World War I subjects. The Abbey eventually put on the play in 1936, but the angry O'Casey exiled himself from Ireland forever.

O'Casey wrote many more plays after *The Silver Tassie*—fantasies, expressionist dramas, moralities—but he never again penned a play that was a popular and critical success. Several of his later plays and his autobiographies reflect his commitment to socialism and communism. His bad temper, sharp tongue, tactlessness, and critical and fractious nature alienated many colleagues in the theatrical world.

Sean and Eileen spent most of the rest of their lives in Devon, where their children were born and brought up. O'Casey continued to write plays for the London stage, and he worked on his multivolume autobiography until his death in 1964. Although he won awards, his post-Abbey plays were not very popular with London audiences and, according to O'Casey's wishes, were not seen by Dublin audiences.

If any playwright learned from the early O'Casey, it was his fellow Dubliner Brendan Behan, who appreciated O'Casey's work with dialect, his efforts to recognize the existence of the urban poor, and his desire to portray their lives with dignity. Behan also understood and employed the O'Casey technique of blending humor, pathos, and tragedy.

Today, of the playwrights who came into prominence during Lady Gregory and Yeats's tenure at the Abbey, O'Casey is the most frequently performed in Ireland and probably on the world stage.

Plays

Although the central themes of O'Casey's great plays, the Dublin trilogy, are always serious, even tragic, they contain superb dialogue, wonderfully humorous characterizations, and some of the most hilariously comic scenes in modern drama. With his tenement people, all the common people of this sad, frightened, and frightening world, O'Casey shows his great love for and understanding of humanity.

The Shadow of a Gunman (1922)

Set in a Dublin tenement room during the 1920 conflict between Irish guerrillas and the Black and Tans, *The Shadow of a Gunman* is the story of a working-class poet, Donal Davoren, who shares a room with a peddler named Seumas Shields. The other inhabitants of the house believe Donal is a rebel gunman hiding out, but he, basking in unearned respect and prestige, does not correct their assumptions. Like many if not most of the author's male characters, the poet and the peddler are lazy cowards, and their lives are essentially aimless; it is the women of the plays who have courage and energy. To save Donal, Minnie Powell, a young worker in the tenement, removes bombs left in the room by a rebel, and she is shot by the Black and Tans. The men live on to stew in their shame and ignominy.

The Shadow of a Gunman indicates the beginnings of O'Casey's superb characterizations and his comic gifts. Donal and Seumas, who wait and cringe instead of taking action, are among the forerunners of Vladimir and Estragon in *Waiting for Godot*.

Written when the War of Independence had just concluded, the play evidences O'Casey's commitment to truth and his personal political courage, even to the extent that Donal, the craven poet, seems to be something of a self-portrait.

Juno and the Paycock (1924)

O'Casey's masterpiece, *Juno and the Paycock*, is set contemporaneously in a Dublin slum flat inhabited by the Boyle family. "Captain" Jack Boyle is the "paycock" who detests work and who lies, brags, and prefers drinking to all other activities. His sidekick is the parasitic Joxer Daly. They are a team, like a harmful Laurel and Hardy, and they have their theater ancestry in the Miles Glorious and Wily Slave of Plautus's Roman comedy.

Jack's wife, Juno, is a magnificent woman, a rock onto whom all the members of a collapsing family cling. She is compassionate and courageous. Her lot is sad, even tragic, but she knows what is right and who is worth saving.

Juno and the Paycock is a play about human wastage that is presented as comic as well as tragic. In it, O'Casey portrays human greatness in the face of great grief, suffering, and hopelessness. Juno and Jack Boyle have two grown but hard-luck children. Johnny was wounded as a guerrilla in the War of Independence, but after the peace treaty he joined the IRA rebels fighting the new Irish government. Now he is crippled, in pain, and frightened because he has betrayed the rebels. They come for the traitor and execute him.

The daughter, Mary, drops her Irish lover for an Englishman, who eventually gets her pregnant and then deserts her. Meanwhile, Jack has been led to believe he has an inheritance coming from the estate of a deceased cousin, and he spends the money before he has it in hand, only to learn that the Englishman's incompetence in drawing up the cousin's will has invalidated the inheritance. Jack now has creditors breathing down his neck and reclaiming his foolish purchases.

Mary is reviled by her father, and her Irish lover, eager to take her back until he learns she is pregnant, will not stand by her. It is Juno who comforts and supports her daughter. And when Johnny is executed, she has to view his body, while Jack and Joxer remain behind, engaged in drunken reverie. The men's comic banter is one of the great pleasures of the play, even though they contribute to "the terrible state o' chassis" in their society. O'Casey implies that masculine vanity, drinking, and foolishness are the curses on Irish womanhood. The family is destroyed, but Juno and Mary will endure and survive, for it is matriarchy that sustains and preserves the race. Unlike the men, Juno is not political. She has no ideology. She is a pragmatic, compassionate human being who is well named after the goddess.

The Plough and the Stars (1926)

Like the other plays in the Dublin trilogy, *The Plough and the Stars* is the story of ordinary people caught up in political events that are far beyond their control. The title comes from the symbols on the flag of the Irish Transport and General Workers' Union, of which O'Casey was once a member. The flag was present at the Easter Rising and was used by the Irish Citizens Army. The title also reflects O'Casey's worker background and identification as well as his lifelong socialism. The play is drawn on a larger scale than the preceding pieces in the Dublin trilogy. Unlike its predecessors, it has several settings: two rooms in a tenement flat, the street, and a pub. In the order of historical events, however, it precedes them; *The Plough and the Stars* takes place in the months just before the 1916 Easter Rising, which at the time O'Casey wrote the play not only had been recognized as a great turning point in Irish history, but had also taken on mythical proportions as a pageant of patriotism. O'Casey attempts to deflate this mythification by showing that the real heroes, the people of greater courage, are those whose instinctive sympathy and compassion cause them to act kindly, generously, and unselfishly.

Zola-like, O'Casey presents a house full of distinct, interesting, well-drawn, and sometimes comic characters in a play that is more tragedy than comedy. The young couple Nora and Jack Clitheroe are expecting a child. He is a commandant in the Citizens Army, which is to fight the British. She attempts to dissuade him from accepting the post but fails as he places honor and patriotism over family. Of course, he is killed in the rising, and Nora loses the baby and her mind. Other characters are more memorable, especially the ever-talking Fluther Good, another Joxer Daly kind of character, and the alcoholic Protestant evangelist Bessie Burgess, who dies heroically when she is cut down by a stray bullet while shielding Nora.

Nationalism and nationalist organizations are satirized by rowdy scenes in the pub, looting during the Rising, and the prostitute Rose

Redmond's scalding indictment of all. In the end, while most of the inhabitants of the slum are cowering in a room, the surviving rebels are led away to prison accompanied by two British soldiers who sing, ironically enough, "Keep the Home Fires Burning."

In proportions almost a pageant, *The Plough and the Stars* had great theatrical impact. Its antiheroic stance catches perfectly the mood of most Western nations in the 1920s as their populations refuted the war fever and mindless chauvinism that led Europe to self-destruct from 1914 through 1918. O'Casey embraced this anti-war disposition and applied it to the heroics of Easter 1916, which, in his view, led to the wasted blood of the War of Independence and the very dirty Irish Civil War.

The Silver Tassie (1929)

In keeping with his antiwar, antinationalism philosophy, one shared with Shaw, O'Casey wrote the impressionistic *The Silver Tassie*. Rejected by the Abbey, *The Silver Tassie* had its first production in London. The "tassie" is a silver cup awarded to a star football (soccer) player, Harry Heegan, at the height of his career, before the Great War leaves him disabled. In the first act, O'Casey shows Heegan in his athletic glory. The second act shows him in battle. In the third and fourth act, he is in a wheelchair, paralyzed. At a dance he cannot participate in, he destroys the silver tassie out of frustration and anger.

In O'Casey's previous plays, minor characters enrich the texture, speaking the crisp dialogue that is so characteristic of O'Casey's and the Abbey's best work. They often embody the play's humor. In *The Silver Tassie,* however, the minor characters are two dimensional, and their language is equally flat.

The second act, set on the battlefield of northern France, is a powerful piece of expressionist-surrealist theater and a brilliant visual poem of despair, but it does not fit in stylistically with the rest of the drama. Unfortunately, in this play O'Casey let his powerful ideas overcome his dramaturgical instincts and become propaganda. *The Silver Tassie* was and is too "arty" for many, especially after the earthy verisimilitude of the Dublin trilogy.

Additional Reading

Hunt, Hugh. *Sean O'Casey*. Dublin: Gill and Macmillan, 1980.

Krause, David. *Sean O'Casey: The Man and His Work*. Rev. ed. New York: Macmillan, 1975.

Murray, Christopher. *Sean O'Casey: Writer at Work*. Dublin: Gill and Macmillan, 2004.

O'Casey, Sean. *Collected Plays*. 4 vols. London: Macmillan, 1949–51.

O'Connor, Gary. *Sean O'Casey: A Life*. New York: Atheneum, 1988.

ALONG WITH O'CASEY

Several other excellent Irish dramatists also contributed to the continuity of the Irish theater during the period dominated by Sean O'Casey. They include Paul Vincent Carroll, Denis Johnston, and M. J. Molloy. Their plays are seldom performed today, but in their time they were popular dramatists on the Irish stage as well as in Britain and America.

PAUL VINCENT CARROLL (1900–1968)

Born at Blackrock, near Dundalk, County Louth, Paul Carroll Vincent was educated at St. Mary's College, Dundalk, and St. Patrick's Training College, Dublin. He immigrated to Scotland when he was twenty-one years old to pursue a career in education. During sixteen years as a Glasgow teacher, he achieved enough writing success to pursue a playwriting career. Carroll's first Abbey play was *Things That Are Caesar's* (1932). His first international success was *Shadow and Substance* (1937). It and *The White Steed* (1939) won major awards in New York.

In 1945, Carroll moved permanently to England, where he continued to write plays as well as film and television scripts. He died in Bromley, Kent. Carroll is perhaps best remembered for his portraits of clergy and the clerical life in his plays. Although he was accused of anticlericalism, his target was not the priesthood itself, but the abuse of power and authority, a perennial theme in modern Irish drama from Synge to the present.

Plays

Shadow and Substance (1937)

A paean to humanity's best virtues—goodness, love, and faith—*Shadow and Substance* portrays two proud men in conflict over the values they represent: Canon Skerritt and the schoolmaster Dermot O'Flingsley. O'Flingsley advises a good-hearted servant girl, Brigid, who sees a vision of her namesake saint, to speak to the canon, but the canon does not treat her seriously. After she is accidentally killed in a brawl, both men comprehend that they share some responsibility for her death. Carroll points out the shortcomings of these hubristic men, who outwardly appear to be pillars of society.

The conflict between the two men goes back to O'Flingsley's publication of a book that the canon finds subversive and wants to use to get O'Flingsley dismissed. Brigid's death brings them together, making them realize not only that their enmity is dangerous, but also that they share moral responsibilities. The play has the subtlety of John Galsworthy's plays—dramas without heroes and with complicated and shifting perspectives.

The White Steed (1939)

In *The White Steed*, a kind, likable, fair-minded canon, Matt Lavelle, who is confined to a wheelchair, battles his younger curate, Father Shaughnessy, a puritan sorely afflicted with self-righteousness and narrowness. In the end, a woman once more facilitates reconciliation and redemption. Nora Fintry, a librarian, helps the canon to educate and humanize the curate. *The White Steed* does not play or read as saccharine as its summation sounds.

Additional Reading

Carroll, Paul Vincent. *Shadows and Substance*. New York: Random House, 1937.

———. *Three Plays: The White Steed; Things That Are Caesar's; and The Strings, My Lord, Are False*. London: Macmillan, 1944.

Doyle, Paul A. *Paul Vincent Carroll*. Lewisburg, Pa.: Bucknell Univ. Press, 1971.

DENIS JOHNSTON (1901–1984)

William Denis Johnston was born in Dublin, the son of a man who would later sit on the bench of the Supreme Court of Ireland. After early education in Dublin and Edinburgh, Johnston studied law at Cambridge University and Harvard University. He practiced law for ten years after being called to the bar in Dublin, Belfast, and London.

Johnston also began to write for the theater, in which he had become interested while at Harvard. He ultimately became a protégé of Shaw and Yeats, but his first play, *Shadowdance*, was rejected by the Abbey with the sentence "The Old Lady Says 'No'" written on the title page, referring to the fact that Lady Gregory had disapproved. Johnston accordingly changed the title to *The Old Lady Says "No!"* He knew his revenge would annoy Lady Gregory and the Abbey Theatre, and it did. The play had a successful production in 1929 at the Gate.

His next play, *The Moon on the Yellow River*, based on the troubles between Republicans and the Irish Free State after the Civil War, was accepted by the Abbey and produced there in 1931, but it was not as successful as its predecessor. Johnston had nine plays professionally performed, most notably *The Golden Cuckoo* (1939), an attack on the blindness of the judicial system.

Johnston worked as a producer for the BBC in Belfast, as a wartime journalist, and then as a teacher in American colleges and universities. As a dramatist, he always expected his audience to rethink—along with him—issues and questions of morality and nationalism.

He was married twice, first to Shelah Richards, then to Betty Chancellor. The novelist Jennifer Johnston is his daughter. He died on 8 August 1984 in Ballybrack, County Dublin.

A highly imaginative playwright who moved from experimentalism to realism in his dramatic writing as well as a man of high intelligence, Johnston was perhaps too cerebral in his work for the theater. A little more emotion may have brought him closer to O'Casey's achievement in the Dublin trilogy, but Johnston probably didn't want to go quite that way, even when he changed his style to realism.

Plays

The Old Lady Says "No!" (1929)

An experimental play and a director's play of many scenes, *The Old Lady Says "No!"* opens with a playlet concerning the Irish martyr Robert Emmet, leader of the unsuccessful 1803 revolt, who made one of Ireland's greatest speeches at his trial. But Johnston's play is not a historical play extolling Irish nationalism. It is really an expressionist satire on language and how it wears out, unable in the end to serve either the past or the present.

After the opening sequence, in which Emmet is knocked unconscious by the British, the play continues in his mind as he makes an appearance in twentieth-century Dublin looking for his sweetheart, Sarah Curran. He plays many roles and in Brechtian fashion reminds the audience that they are watching theater, not life. Modern Irish life is presented as squalid, disjointed, and aimless, having been torn loose from the moorings of the past, and the heady nationalism of the 1920s is given a stiff working over—in the manner of O'Casey—that verges on political blasphemy.

Additional Reading

Barnett, Gene A. *Denis Johnston*. Boston: Twayne, 1980.
Johnston, Denis. *The Dramatic Works of Denis Johnston*. 2 vols. Toronto: Macmillan, 1977.

M. J. MOLLOY (1917–1994)

Born in Milltown, County Galway, Michael Joseph Molloy trained for the priesthood but was deflected from his vocation by tuberculosis. He began writing plays in the hospital. Molloy spent most of his life farming near Milltown. As a writer, he embraced the language and the folklore of Ireland's West in a fashion approaching that of Synge. He wrote effectively about the experiences of ordinary Irish people, including the outcasts such as peddlers and travelers.

His first play performed at the Abbey, *The Old Road* (1943), focuses on the depopulation of Ireland's western provinces because of emigration and the lure of the cities. Molloy's finest play is *The King of Friday's Men* (1948). These dramas are distinctively his; there is no mistaking his themes of social disruption and his direct style (much like that of a folk play) for anyone else's. His reclusive life allowed him to concentrate his art on the rural environment in which he lived, the people he spent his life with, and the legends they shared.

Plays

The King of Friday's Men (1948)
A nostalgic drama, *The King of Friday's Men* is part of Molloy's romantic lament for the long-gone Ireland of the preindustrial age.

Though set in the eighteenth century, it recalls heroes of the Celtic past when its hero, Bartley Dowd, destroys a lord's contingent of men with a few bashes from his wide-swinging shillelagh. In this drama, western Irish society in Galway and Mayo is still in the grip of hierarchical feudalism, lords on top and peasants on bottom. The lord, Caesar French, demands his right to make mistresses of his peasants' daughters. Forced to provide him with one, they choose a betrothed girl, Una Brehony, for the sexual sacrifice, but she is defended by Bartley Dowd.

Caesar French's droit du seigneur and treachery cause havoc in the country and bring about French's death at Dowd's hands. The old order is passing, and its rulers are slow to comprehend the fact. In its epic range and melodramatic energy, the drama reads and plays like a work of Sir Walter Scott.

The Paddy Pedlar (1952)

Molloy's popular one-act play *The Paddy Pedlar* is a macabre comedy that has as its background the beginning of the famine decade, the 1840s. A thieving, roguish trickster named Ooshla Clancy has cheated a young girl, Honor, of her inheritance and tries, with an accomplice, to rob a peddler of what he thinks are stolen riches in the man's sack. But it turns out that in the sack the peddler is carrying his mother's body to her old home for burial. Shocked at the sight of a corpse instead of the expected loot, Ooshla gives his farm to Honor and her fiancé and goes off with the peddler, who will keep him on the straight and narrow with knife pricks, but who, as a "gentleman" peddler, charges twice what his goods are worth. Black humor is the only way to describe this devilishly clever morality play.

Additional Reading

Hogan, Robert. "Michael Molloy's Dying Ireland." In *After the Irish Renaissance*. London: Macmillan, 1968.

Molloy, M. J. *The King of Friday's Men*. Dublin: James Duffy, 1953.
O'Driscoll, Robert. *Selected Plays of M. J. Molloy*. Washington, D.C.: Catholic Univ. of America Press, 1998.

SAMUEL BECKETT (1906–1989)

Samuel Barclay Beckett was born into an affluent Protestant family of mercantile Huguenot origins, in Foxrock, one of Dublin's fashionable southern suburbs. He was the second son and last child of William Beckett, a successful surveyor who worked in the building industry as a cost estimator and a materials facilitator, and Maria (May) Jones Roe Beckett, who had nursed at the hospital in which William Beckett was briefly a patient. Young Samuel (called Sam) had elementary schooling between the ages of five to nine at the Misses Elsners' Academy near Foxrock. There he began his intense study of French that continued throughout his formal education. From his ninth through his thirteenth year, he studied in Dublin as a commuter student at the Earlsfort School. In 1920, he was sent north to study at the Eton-like Portora Royal School in Enniskillen, County Fermanagh, and then he entered Trinity College, Dublin, majoring in modern languages. He graduated with a bachelor of arts degree in 1927, and he accepted a position teaching French in Belfast at Campbell College, a prestigious public school. Although Beckett later returned to Trinity College as a lecturer in French and subscribed for his master's degree in 1931, he intensely disliked teaching.

In 1929, he went to Paris to work as a lecturer in the École normale supérieure. In the French capital, which in the Jazz Age was the avant-garde capital of Western culture, he met and was befriended by James Joyce, who became his mentor. Beckett helped Joyce, whose eyesight was failing, in any way he could, primarily as a reader, although he occasionally took dictation and did research. Unfortunately, Joyce's mentally disturbed daughter, Lucia, fell in love with Beckett, and his rejection of her added to her difficulties.

The Joyce family felt Beckett had led Lucia on, though he had not, so cordial relations between the Joyces and the young writer ceased for a time. Nevertheless, James Joyce would always remain a great—perhaps the greatest—linguistic influence on the younger author.

During 1929, Beckett began to publish in magazines, and then his long poem *Whorescope* appeared in book form, followed by his study *Proust*. Returning to Ireland in 1930, he taught French at Trinity, hoping to please his family with a conventional job. But he still hated teaching, and so he walked out on the lectureship and promptly fled back to Paris to escape both Trinity and his pious and difficult mother, with whom he had a love-hate relationship. His infrequent visits to Ireland were always traumatic for the sensitive writer.

In 1932, Beckett returned home again, ill and destitute, to obtain medical treatment and to write. For the first time, he consciously eschewed realism in his creative writing. The next year his beloved and generous father died unexpectedly, but Beckett's *More Pricks Than Kicks,* a story collection, was accepted by Chatto and Windus. It was his first significant publication in fiction. Chronically depressed and wracked with psychosomatic illnesses, however, he underwent psychoanalytic treatment in London from 1933 to 1935, where he read extensively in psychology and heard Carl Jung lecture.

The years up through 1937, when he was writing *Murphy* (1938), his first published novel, were peripatetic ones for him as he moved, in continual ill health, between London and the family home, Cooldrinagh, in Foxrock. He also had an extended sojourn in Germany to study the language and art, mostly contemporary painting (the painter Jack Yeats was one of his good friends), and to see what was happening to that nation under the repugnant Nazis. After a final break with his smothering mother in 1937, Beckett moved to Paris, the city that he would make his home for the remainder of his life.

When France was overrun by the Germans in World War II, Beckett committed himself to France, although Eire was neutral, and he courageously joined the French Resistance in 1941. Betrayed along with others in his Resistance unit, he had to flee Paris to hide from the Gestapo in the village of Roussillon (d'Apt) in the Vaucluse, about thirty miles from Avignon, laboring through 1944 as an agricultural worker until U.S. troops liberated the village. In 1945, he joined the staff of the Irish Red Cross hospital at St.-Lô. For his services to France, he was awarded the Croix de guerre and the Médaille de la reconnaissance after the war.

Beckett's major novels were either written in French and translated by himself into English or written in English and translated into French: *Murphy* (1938), *Watt* (written during World War II and published in 1953), *Molloy* (1951), *The Unnamable* (1953), *Malone Dies* (1957), and *How It Is* (1961). All are philosophical works in which Beckett moves from logical positivism to deep, despairing existentialism. It is in his novels, especially the earlier ones, and in his story collection *More Pricks than Kicks* (1934) that Joyce's influence is most apparent. Unlike Joyce but like Sartre, Beckett was a secularist, disinterested in myth. He embraced phenomenology. All we get is what we see—namely, this world through our imperfect senses. Nothing transcends the boundaries of human experience.

Waiting for Godot (1954), first written in French as *En attendant Godot* (1952), is Beckett's dramatic masterpiece, a profound statement on the human condition. This minimalist experimental play, which more than any other play influenced twentieth-century European and American drama, seemed for a while to have put an end to realism on the stage and the conventions of the well-made play: exposition, complication, resolution. It was the work that led to Beckett's Nobel Prize for Literature in 1969. The seriocomic ambiguity and puzzling symbolic wordplay of *Godot,* in part inspired by the dramaturgy of Eugéne Ionesco, Jean Genet, and Arthur Adamov, foreshadow the plays of Edward Albee, Harold Pinter, Tom

Stoppard, and others in the movement referred to as the "theater of the absurd."

Endgame, a one-act play, appeared in 1958, having first been written as *Fin de partie* a year earlier. *Acte sans paroles* (1957), a mime play, became *Act Without Words* (1958). The one-act dramatic monologue *Krapp's Last Tape* (1958), written for the Irish actor Pat Magee, is one of Beckett's most frequently performed dramas. The ironically titled *Happy Days* appeared in 1961 and was the last of Beckett's major dramas, although he continued to write plays with diminishing dialogue and lessening action for fifteen more years.

Beckett's plays are more theater than drama. They support performance, pushing it to the foreground. They are spectacular in the sense that the audience learns almost as much from looking as from listening. The actor's business in Beckett's dramas is often slapstick, demonstrating the effect that silent film comedians such as Charley Chaplin and Buster Keaton had on his work. Vladimir and Estragon did not evolve far from Chaplin's Little Tramp. The plays, however, are not mere spectacles: they also become vehicles for multiple "readings." Each member of the audience or each reader sees and feels the play, making an individual interpretation of it, responding to the simple but profound words as the archetypal scenes flood the senses.

After World War II, Beckett, except for occasional trips, spent the rest of his life in Paris and in a modest country cottage in Ussy, a village forty miles from the city. Although he had turned down many honors, in 1959 he accepted an honorary doctor of letters degree from Trinity. In 1961, he married his lover and companion of more than twenty years, Suzanne Deschevaux-Dumesnil, in order to secure an inheritance for her. He accepted the Nobel Prize for Literature in 1969 but did not attend the award ceremony in Stockholm. He and his wife felt the award was a disaster because the notoriety impinged on his writing time and their privacy.

As his fame grew, he became more and more reclusive and secretive. His friends tended more to be artists and theater people than writers. Continuing habits he began in early manhood, he drank copious amounts of Irish whiskey and smoked heavily.

Up to the last few weeks of his life, Beckett continued to write. After a stay in Le Tiers Temps, a nursing home, Samuel Beckett died of emphysema and Parkinson's disease on 22 December 1989 in the Hôpital Saint-Anne. Suzanne had died a few months earlier, on 17 July, and he was buried next to her. They had no children.

Plays

Waiting for Godot (1954)

Waiting for Godot is the great twentieth-century play of inquiring—of skeptical seeking for a meaning for life, of questioning not the existence of God, but the existence of existence. As a minimalist work, it reduces human life to its fundamental pain and its few and small pleasures. Waiting is the being and the end in itself, the only process. And we wait within the prison of our senses. We are alone: that is the essential (or existential) fact of the human condition.

Human beings continue in nihilistic futility, acting irrationally and not realizing the impossibility of real communication between themselves. The protagonists—two tramps, Vladimir and Estragon—have only their suffering to prove they are alive and only their frail friendship to comfort them. Their world—our world as audience—is an almost featureless barren plain. It might as well be the moon except for its one, leafless tree. The tramps are waiting for someone named Godot to rescue them from their misery. But Godot does not come. Instead, a cruel, whip-wielding master, Pozzo, and his demented former teacher and now slave, Lucky, tethered on a long rope, arrive and stay a short while. Their pause gives Pozzo the opportunity to smoke his pipe, talk about selling Lucky, and give him a kick and then a handkerchief when he sobs. Finally, they leave as they came, roped together by Lucky's long tether. At the end of the act, a messenger boy arrives, purportedly from Godot, announcing that Godot will come tomorrow.

The second act finds the tree showing five leaves and the tramps continuing the unending process of waiting. Pozzo and Lucky return and collapse; now Pozzo is blind, and Lucky is unable to speak. The tramps help Pozzo up. Lucky will not take advantage of the situation to reverse roles. Pozzo goads him on, and they exit as they had entered. The messenger arrives again and once more states that Godot will come tomorrow. The tramps question him about Godot to no avail, and he exits. The tramps then try to hang themselves but fail. With nightfall, they decide to meet again the next day to wait for Godot. Agreeing to leave, they stay. The tragicomedy ends.

It is for the audience to ask and answer its own questions: Where are the tramps, and why are they there? What is their relationship? Who is Godot? Does he really exist? Is the messenger telling the truth? What is the meaning of the suddenly blooming tree? What is the significance of the Pozzo–Lucky relationship? Is there any resolution or closure to this stark play, punctuated with black humor? Why can't they go? Why can't they let go?

Waiting for Godot is Samuel Beckett's vision of the inner universe, the human mind in the brief interval between the womb and the tomb. The play foreshadows the end of hope. We wait with Vladimir and Estragon in hopeless hope for the play to end and for life to end. Waiting is the human condition. But if we are waiting for something, someone—Godot or God—we are deceived either by ourselves or by bourgeois society. The existential credo is not the Cartesian "I think, therefore I am," but instead "I suffer, therefore I am."

Endgame (1958)

The one-act play *Endgame* is also about waiting, and just as *Waiting for Godot* is about the never-to-be-fulfilled promise of a salvational arrival, *Endgame* is about the never-to-be-fulfilled promise of a salvational departure. The "endgame" is the last part of a chess game, so the play is the endgame of life as death approaches.

Endgame is set in a bare interior with two small, high-up windows. The room may be the skull or the brain, and the windows the eyes, but with nothing to see. Sitting in the middle of the room in a wheelchair is a blind old man, Hamm. He is unable to stand. He wears a scarlet dressing gown that looks like a cardinal's robe, and he has a skullcap on his head and a blood-soaked handkerchief over his face. His servant, Clov, is standing by the door as the curtain rises. He is unable to sit and can only totter. Hamm and Clov, like Pozzo and Lucky, are bound to each other.

Also on the stage, standing near the wall, are two ash cans, containing Hamm's elderly, legless parents, Nag and Nell, who have lost their legs in a tandem bicycle accident. The characters believe that they are the sole survivors of a great catastrophe. Thus, the play is about the end of all human life. Hamm, like Pozzo, is vicious and selfish. Clov would like to leave but cannot. Like Lucky, he is irrevocably tied to a cruel master, and the tension of the drama stems from the question of Clov's ability to free himself. Hamm has the last food left in the world but cannot feed himself. If Clov leaves, Hamm starves, but so will Clov. No one can escape the cruel relationships of life: lord and peasant, capitalist and worker, sadist and masochist, wife and husband, friend and enemy, and other binaries.

Near the end of the play, Clov looks out of the windows and to his surprise sees a small boy through his telescope. He wonders: "A potential procreator?" But Hamm sums up human despairing indifference: "If he exists he'll die there or he'll come here." Hamm again covers his face, and Clov continues to wait.

With the verbal economy of a modern poem, Beckett has moved humans into their skulls. Action has become meaningless, if it ever had meaning, and the values of Western culture—God, art, family, nation, and love—have no existential reality.

Krapp's Last Tape (1958)

Written for the Irish actor Patrick Magee, *Krapp's Last Tape* is the most popular of Beckett's shorter plays. This one-act monologue is the author's most "Irish play" in that Krapp is clearly an old Irishman, addicted to bananas, listening to his own voice recounting his younger days on his tape recorder, and trying to bridge time. Nearly deaf and blind and limping badly, the alcoholic sixty-nine-year-old man listens to a recording he made on his thirty-ninth birthday in which the voice recalls a love affair he had in his late twenties.

We learn of the death of his mother and the end of his last love affair. He tries to record another story, but his mind wanders off into the realm of vague recollections of his writing career and the mere parody of a love affair. He stops recording and plays "thirty-nine" again, allowing the tape to run out into silence as the play concludes. "The rest is silence."

Krapp's Last Tape is not sentimental; it is metaphysical. Krapp is seeking understanding, meaning, knowledge. Beckett chronicles the artist's need to represent his life through the structure of events. Krapp looks for his identity in the eyes of his love, and when he asks her, "Let me in," his plea is not merely sexual, but a forlorn attempt to establish his existence through the power of their relationship.

Happy Days (1961)

Of course, the title is ironic—there are no happy days in Beckett Land. The two-act play *Happy Days* presents the most profound female character in Beckett's oeuvre: Winnie, buried like a prehistoric goddess up to her breasts in the earth.

A "happy day" occurs in the first act, when there is a little less suffering and pain. Winnie is waiting not for redemption or escape, but for a bell to ring. Like the bell of the mass or the summoning of the Angelus or the signal for Pavlov's dog, the ringing will allow her to sleep away the remainder of her life. Next to death, sleep is the preferable condition for humans. Winnie prays, brushes her teeth, spits, and tries without success to communicate with her silent, unseen husband, Willie. She is running out of stores: toothpaste, petroleum jelly, and words.

In the second act, Winnie is embedded up to her neck. Things are worse. She no longer prays. She is barely able to understand the meaning of her fragmented phrases and words. As the play nears conclusion, Willie crawls into sight and gropes his way to the pile in which Winnie is buried, but he can't quite reach her. With his last energy, he mutters, "Win." Enraptured by this overwhelmingly "joyous" event, Winnie bursts into the female part of the waltz duet in *The Merry Widow* as the curtain falls.

Beckett's irony in *Happy Days* is almost unbearable. Human beings are sinking even as they embrace the illusion of love and mutter worn-out words. Winnie and Willie's companionship is absurd, futile, grotesque, and pathetic, yet it is also somehow touching, for what else is there? Perhaps the happy ending to Beckett's last major work is the thought that there is an a priori value after all: human companionship can slightly assuage the pain of human existence, and in the frozen winter of the world one suffers a bit less if another person is with one. So much for the human condition.

Additional Reading

Beckett, Samuel. *Collected Works.* 16 vols. New York: Grove Press, 1970.

————. *Endgame, a Play in One Act.* New York: Grove Press, 1958; London: Faber and Faber, 1958.

————. *Happy Days.* New York: Grove Press, 1961; London: Faber and Faber, 1962.

————. *Krapp's Last Tape.* London: Faber and Faber, 1959; New York: Grove Press, 1960.

————. *Waiting for Godot.* New York: Grove Press, 1954; London: Faber and Faber, 1956.

Ben-Zvi, Linda. *Samuel Beckett.* Boston: Twayne, 1986.

Bloom, Harold. *Samuel Beckett.* New York: Chelsea House, 1985.

Knowlson, James. *Damned to Fame: The Life of Samuel Beckett.* New York: Simon and Schuster, 1996.

BRENDAN BEHAN (1923–1964)

A beloved writer who personified the strengths and weaknesses of many Irishmen, Brendan Francis Behan seemed to win the hearts of Irish people in general and of Dubliners in particular. Behan, the son of a house painter, left school (Sisters of Charity on William Street and the Brunswick Street Christian Brothers Seminary) to work in the trade. He was also "schooled" by frequent attendance at the Queen's Theatre and Dublin music halls.

Like his father, a Republican activist who was once imprisoned, Behan joined the IRA. Almost immediately, in December 1939, he was arrested by British police in Liverpool for possessing explosives and sentenced as a juvenile to three years in Borstal, a juvenile detention center. Behan was released in December 1941 and returned home to Dublin, only to be arrested again in April for shooting at an Irish detective at a political funeral. This time he was sentenced to fourteen years, serving his time in several prisons, including Mountjoy Prison in Dublin.

While incarcerated, he read voraciously, and he learned Irish from fellow inmates. After general amnesty in 1946 brought about his early release, he moved to the West—County Kerry and County Connemara—to attempt to stay out of trouble and to begin a writing career. Returning to Dublin, he was able to make his living with his pen, writing stories and articles for Radio Eireann and the *Irish Press.*

Behan wrote several stage plays but could not get them performed. His first play to receive a stage production was *The Quare Fellow,* which the Abbey had turned down. Produced instead by Alan Simpson in November 1954 at the Pike Theatre, it proved an outstanding success, and from that time to the end of his life

Behan was a Dublin celebrity. Marriage to Beatrice Salkeld followed the next year. When the avant-garde British theater director Joan Littlewood presented *The Quare Fellow* in London in 1956, Behan acquired an international reputation. His next playwriting success was *An Giall,* in Irish, for Gael-Linn at the Damer Theatre in 1958. Translated as *The Hostage,* the play was another resounding success when Littlewood produced it in London later that year. Next came Behan's autobiography, *Borstal Boy* (1958), a portrait of the artist as a young prisoner.

Now Behan, who was surely one of the world's greatest conversationalists, was in demand all over Europe and America as a guest on television talk shows. His two major plays were in constant production around the globe. His later unfinished play, *Richard's Cork Leg,* completed by Alan Simpson and first produced in 1972 has not been successful, but Frank McMahon's brilliant adaptation of *Borstal Boy* for the stage in 1967 created, in effect, another Behan play, one frequently performed and very popular. Behan also wrote several witty and insightful books, including *Brendan Behan's Island* (1962) and *Brendan Behan's New York* (1964).

Tragically, the once poor youth from the Dublin tenements turned perpetual roaring boy couldn't handle his success. Drunkenness and diabetes ruined his health and his life. It was a sloppy life, but one of meteoric achievement. He died in Dublin on 20 March 1964 at the age of forty-one. His funeral was gigantic, and the illegal IRA gave him a soldier's burial. It seemed that all Dublin felt the loss and came out to say farewell to a man they all related to as a beloved personal friend.

In the four years of Behan's high creativity, 1954 through 1958, he reinvigorated the Irish stage with the language of the Dublin working class and with the ironic humor and sardonic wisdom of the disbelieving underprivileged who know that they are born outcasts and that their resistance to authority is ultimately futile— but what the hell! Behan's plays are yet another expression of the ordinary Irish experience. Like O'Casey, he gave voice to the Dublin poor, and his plays, in their way, are as political as O'Casey's, depicting common people whose fate is determined by economic forces beyond their control as they are swept up in historical conflicts they barely comprehend.

Plays

The Quare Fellow (1954)

A brilliant and deeply moving protest against capital punishment, *The Quare Fellow* is set in Mountjoy Prison, Dublin, "on the banks of the Royal Canal." Here prisoners and warders are caught up in a culture of oppression and must cope as best they can. The play is based on the execution by hanging of a man who had killed his brother. Behan had known the man in Mountjoy. Because Behan, in his IRA days, could have been executed if the shots he fired at police or the explosives he carried had killed anyone, *The Quare Fellow* might have been his way of coming to terms with his nightmares about this possibility.

The protagonist, the Quare Fellow, who is continually spoken of and then hanged, never appears, yet he is amazingly a very real character indeed. For both the play's characters and the audience, the great suspense of the play is in the waiting for the execution. A prisoner reprieved at the last moment doesn't know what to do with his life, and so he tries to kill himself. Filled with black humor and thematic song, the play is ultimately about human relationships and identity, reduced in the prison to a card on the cell printed with a name, a religion, and the length of the sentence—in other words, the roll call of life itself.

The Hostage (1958)

The setting of *The Hostage* is a brothel. Once again Behan, like O'Casey, reduces national issues to the level of the individual human beings who are caught up in great issues. But unlike O'Casey, Behan mocks these issues with his jumble of styles, dance, music hall business, and song.

An IRA operative has been captured and is about to be executed in Northern Ireland; in reprisal, an English soldier has been seized and taken to Dublin as a hostage. The brothel is run by a former IRA man but is owned by an Englishman who speaks Irish. The captive soldier falls in love with an Irish servant girl, and the audience hopes love will conquer hatred, but in the end he is executed. His death is more important to Behan than all the issues contested, for Behan's sympathy and compassion is always with the individual. Brendan Behan was a big man with a big soul. His compassion for his fellow humans shines through his drama and his prose.

Additional Reading

Behan, Brendan. *Borstal Boy*. London: Methuen, 1958; New York: Knopf, 1959.

———. *Complete Plays*. New York: Grove Press, 1978.

Boyle, Ted E. *Brendan Behan*. Boston: Twayne, 1969.

Kearney, Colbert. *The Writings of Brendan Behan*. Dublin: Gill and Macmillan, 1977.

O'Connor, Ulick. *Brendan Behan*. London: Hamish Hamilton, 1970.

O'Sullivan, Michael. *Brendan Behan: A Life*. Boulder, Colo.: Roberts Rhinehart, 1999.

9

Brian Friel and Other Modern Dramatists

AT THIS WRITING (2010), Brian Friel is the most important living Irish dramatist, a world-famous playwright who has won the championship belt previously worn by Synge, O'Casey, and Beckett. But Ireland is also blessed with an extraordinary number of outstanding playwrights besides Brian Friel. The depth, range, and quality of currant dramatic activity is professionally unsurpassed in any other Western country, regardless of size. Contemporary with Friel, although some are now deceased, is a pantheon of remarkable writers with international reputations who bring honor to the nation.

BRIAN FRIEL (B. 1929)

A production of a new Brian Friel play is international news. Revivals around the world bring forth new admirers. For millions, Friel speaks for Ireland from the stage. Of course, no one today can speak for all of Ireland, but Friel, a Roman Catholic born in Northern Ireland, educated in both the North and the South, and residing in Donegal, not far from the border between the two (sitting on the geographical fence, so to speak), comes closest of all contemporary Irish dramatists to doing so. He is an Ulsterman, and even though he now lives in the Irish Republic, his home in Donegal is in that ancient province of Ulster. Furthermore, the consensus is that *Translations* (1980) is the most significant and profound Irish drama of the postmodern epoch.

Friel was born in Omagh, County Tyrone, where his father taught school. In 1939, when Friel was ten, the family moved to the city of Derry, and he received his early education there: first at the Long Tower School, where his father taught, and then at St. Columb's College. He spent two years at the Catholic seminary at Maynooth College, County Kildare, and received a bachelor's degree, but without intending ordination. In 1948, he enrolled in St. Joseph's Teacher Training College in Belfast and then became a schoolmaster in several primary and intermediary schools in Derry from 1950 to 1960. His first play, *The Francophile,* was staged in 1960 at the Ulster Group Theatre in Belfast; it was later adapted for radio as *A Doubtful Paradise.* His second and third plays were *The Enemy Within* (1962), a history play set in the sixth century on St. Columba's Iona, and *The Blind Mice* (1963), a problem play about loyalties within and without the Catholic Church. Like *The Francophile,* these two works are little regarded today.

During his teaching career, writing after work, Friel had much success as a short-story writer for the *New Yorker* and other magazines, and the BBC produced his radio plays. His short story collections include *The Saucer of Larks* (1962); *The Gold in the Sea* (1966); and *Selected Stories* (1979), which was republished as *The Diviner* (1982). These skillfully crafted stories are about Ireland's North. They sing the nostalgic song of rural loss and mark the transient but precious moments of life as his characters seek a meaning beyond survival.

Marriage to Anne Morrison came in 1954 while Friel was still teaching and struggling to find time to write. The couple has five children. In 1963, Friel traveled to America to observe, work with, and learn from the distinguished Irish and international director Tyrone Guthrie as Guthrie launched what became the Tyrone Guthrie Theatre in Minneapolis. There Friel acquired knowledge of the techniques of skillfully building plays and studied the ways of the professional theater.

The great historical, political, and social event of Friel's life was the resurgence of the "Troubles," beginning in 1968 with marches and countermarches, the breakdown of law and order, the massacre of fourteen Catholic marchers by British soldiers in Derry in 1972, and the continuing terror, reprisals, assassinations, and bombings as Northern Ireland disintegrated into a fearful world of police and soldiers facing off against guerrillas, with the civilian population held hostage to the vast international failure of political imagination and courage. In that maelstrom, Friel's art was at least temporarily politicized.

One result of that politicization was the founding of the Field Day Theatre Company in 1980 by Friel and the actor Stephen Rea in Derry, with the Guildhall as its venue. Its raison d'être was the production of plays that would radicalize audiences and perhaps bring political and social change to Northern Ireland. Field Day, a phenomenon, was an institution that was not restricted entirely to theater, but rather, with Derry as its epicenter, it embraced several cultural facets including publishing. Seamus Heaney, the future Nobel laureate, and Seamus Deane, a noted scholar, were among the Irish luminaries associated with Field Day early on. *Translations* in 1980 was the new northern company's first and greatest production. It should be noted that Friel never exclusively associated with one company. His plays have premiered in the Abbey more than elsewhere, but they have also opened at Dublin's Gaiety, Olympia, and Gate; New York's Helen Hayes Theater and Longacre Theater; and London's Royal Court Theatre and National Theatre.

In 1987, the Republic of Ireland gave Friel the highest recognition it has for an artist: he was appointed to the Irish Senate.

Major plays by Brian Friel include the following in chronological order. *Philadelphia, Here I Come!* (1967), which established Friel's national and international reputations, shows the private and public personae of a young man about to emigrate. *The Loves of Cass*

McGuire (1966) treats the returning of an exile: an old drunken, derelict, embarrassing, unwanted Irish American woman.

The Lovers (1967) includes two stories: "Winners," with two school dropouts—the girl pregnant—dreaming of their future, although they will eventually die in a boating accident; and "Losers," a comedy in which a middle-aged bachelor tries to prevent the mother of the spinster he is wooing from learning of his intentions.

In *Crystal and Fox* (1968), the head of a rundown traveling show, Fox Melarkey, destroys his family, his business, his identity, and his and his wife's life in his vain attempt to recapture an ideal and innocent world.

The Mundy Scheme (1969) has Friel satirically wondering if the republic is actually a nation or a pastoral playground for Europe and America. *The Gentle Island* (1971), symbolically Ireland, is in fact Inishleen, off Donegal's coast, from which most of the islanders are leaving for menial jobs in British cities; the few remaining are caught up in destructive jealousies and feuds.

The Freedom of the City (1973) is Friel's angry reaction to the massacre in 1972. *Volunteers* (1975), like its predecessor, is based on contemporary events, this time in Dublin, where the city council is destroying the Viking archaeological site to build offices, and political prisoners volunteer to work to save what bits of history can be saved, but, with the Irish proclivity for self-destruction, their fellow prisoners brand them traitors and threaten their lives.

Living Quarters (1977), like Euripides' *Hippolytus,* depicts in experimental form the vulnerability and fragility of a family in which the young must either extract understanding and values from uncooperative elders or destroy the unit. *Aristocrats* (1979) is an elegy to the end of the Irish Big House as well as an anatomy of a declining Catholic family. *Faith Healer* (1979) is about a con artist waiting for a miracle, with dire results.

Translations (1980) contains the great theme of the lamented near death of the Irish language. *The Communication Cord* (1982) finds Friel unsentimentalizing Irish rural life, symbolized by a cottage that in the end nature destroys as if in protest against hypocrisy and delusion. *Making History* (1988) deals with the way the future chooses to remember the trials and struggles of the great Irish soldier Hugh O'Neill and the historically pivotal battle of Kinsale in 1601.

Dancing at Lughnasa (1990) is a ritual drama in which the ancient festival of dance and music is reflected in the lives of five unmarried sisters and the unstable men in their lives. *Wonderful Tennessee* (1993) is like a medieval text, with each teller telling her or his personal story, which may only approximate truth. In *Molly Sweeney* (1994), Friel, like Synge in *The Well of the Saints*, examines blindness from the point of view of a woman born into it who is faced with the possibility of partial vision that will change and complicate her life. *Give Me Your Answer, Do!* (1997) is a despairing parable of a novelist's inability to handle the emotional demands on him made by a wife, a mentally handicapped child, relatives, and friends when his own creativity has dried up and financial ruin is imminent.

Friel's most recent plays include *Performances* (2002), which depicts the passion of a great composer in love with a much younger married woman; *Afterplay* (2002), which features two characters from Chekhov plays who are unable to escape what happened earlier in their lives; and *The Home Place* (2005), which presents a widower and his son who are in love with their housekeeper and an English cousin who arrives to complicate relationships.

Important also are Friel's translation/adaptation of Chekhov's *Three Sisters* (1981) and his dramatization of Turgenev's *Fathers and Sons* (1987).

For the most part, Donegal and Derry comprise the environment and inspiration for Friel's plays. This economically depressed region of high unemployment and much emigration is bisected by an artificial dividing line, the boundary between the Irish Republic and the British province of Northern Ireland, where on the Northern Ireland side Roman Catholics have endured discrimination and political repression at least since 1923. Sectarian strife, until recently, simmered and often boiled over.

Friel creates imaginary towns in which he can order events and command fate: Ballybeg (small town) and Ballymore (big town). Ballybeg is a rural town whose old Irish traditions, values, and culture have been continually eroded from the late eighteenth century to the present. It is a town between the cusps of colonialism and postcolonialism.

In a critique of capitalistic and colonial society, Friel's sympathy is with the poor, the dispossessed, the struggling artists, the disenfranchised youths without hope and trapped by the impediments of the past and the crushing weight of institutions. But although Friel's writing is always informed by a sense of historical injustice and imperial oppression and appropriation, there is humor and satire in his work, and the plays are always compassionate. He has tried to remain an observer—to stand above the fray, so to speak—but in the end his compassionate heart, his love for all of Ireland and all the Irish people, and his deeply ingrained loyalty betray and ennoble him.

Plays

Philadelphia, Here I Come! (1967)

Eschewing his usual linear plot, Friel in *Philadelphia, Here I Come!* splits the character of Gar O'Donnell into two roles, his public and his private self—an attention-getting, theatrical device. Set in his home the night before Gar is to emigrate from Ballybeg to America, the play is centered on the relationships that the young man finds difficult to resolve before leaving: his relationship to his beloved town and, more complicated, his relationship to his widowed father, whom he simultaneously mocks, despises, and loves.

The alter ego, a secret sharer, can be heard only by Gar, and thus the sharer is able to say things to—or rather at—people that Gar cannot. Nevertheless, they are one person. Gar's chums arrive to bid farewell, and in their reminiscences they portray the paucity and vacuity of small-town Donegal life: the coldness, the spiritual bankruptcy, the repression, the empty streets, the joylessness, the seductions never achieved, and the empty future.

In the course of the play, Gar's mood shifts. He wants to cast off memories of the past, lighten the emotional baggage he will carry abroad, and bring closure to his relationships with his father, the mothering housekeeper Madge, his old schoolmaster, and the girlfriend who rejected him because her father insisted.

Friel implies that Gar can't really communicate with himself, let alone his father. Gar will go to Philadelphia and live with a mothering, childless aunt, carrying his half-unwanted bag of memories because it is his destiny to leave and lose what he loves and never to love the freedom he has won.

The Aristocrats (1979)

A play reminiscent of Chekhov's *The Cherry Orchard* and Lennox Robinson's *The Big House,* Friel's *Aristocrats* is set within a Big House, Ballybeg Hall, and on its lawns. The inhabitants are not Anglo-Irish "aristocrats," but Roman Catholics. The house belongs to district judge Justice O'Donnell, the third generation of high judicial officials. Called "Father" by his children, he has a startling, commanding voice that is heard in the first two acts through the loudspeaker of a baby alarm intercom set near his upstairs bed so he can be monitored downstairs, for he has had strokes, is partially paralyzed, and is demented.

As in *The Cherry Orchard* and *Uncle Vanya,* an old social order is disintegrating, but here the fault is patriarchy, the power of Father, who has debilitated, stifled, and overcontrolled his children—three daughters and a son—until they have rebelled in various ways: by taking up causes repugnant to him, by having a child out of wed-lock, by joining a nunnery in Africa, by becoming an alcoholic or remaining at home vaguely content to marry a middle-aged, green-grocer widower with four children, or, in the sad case of the son, Casimir, by developing into a self-deluding, fib-telling, timorous, and effete person.

At the end of the second act, Father leaves his bed, collapses, and dies, thus upsetting his youngest daughter's plans to marry. The third act takes place after the funeral. The wedding for which they have assembled is postponed for three months, and they learn that without the judge's pension, the house, which is falling apart, is no longer tenable. As they leave for their various lives and destinations, it is only the husband of the alcoholic daughter who feels a senti-mental loss. Because his family had long worked for the masters of the Big House, he knows that he is losing his inheritance as much as Father's children are losing theirs.

Friel is superb in creating the atmosphere of decay, disintegra-tion, and loss as an epoch and the way of life the Big House sup-ported come to an end. A family has descended the social ladder. There will no longer be Catholic "aristocrats" at Ballybeg House. The world will still go on, though, and the children will survive as best they can. It is in the human spirit to do so. Casimir may have the answer: don't expect much from the world, and you will be safe.

Faith Healer (1979)

Like Akira Kurosawa's *Rashomon*, Friel's *Faith Healer* is narrated from the divergent viewpoints of three characters, each of whom has a spin on shared past events. The play is structured around four monologues: Frank Hardy, the faith healer, offers the first and the last; his wife, Grace, and his manager, Teddy, speak the other two. Frank is a traveling faith healer who is not sure if he has the power. He recollects his successes and failures in traveling through remote areas of England, Wales, and Scotland in a ramshackle caravan, performing each night in small communities, offering the very ill hope of a cure, while waiting for a miracle himself.

Unsure of his effectiveness, he nevertheless is convinced that he responds to real human need. Frank may symbolize Friel the playwright and the doubts that most true artists have about their art, for he, like Friel or any playwright, is a creator of lives, albeit fictions. He writes the scenario for his own death at the hands of his people as if he were a mythic old god turned scapegoat, for death, like faith, waits at home for the exile's return. Frank achieves the peace he has sought, but Grace, who has never gotten over the loss of their stillborn child and is unable to live without the power of the faith healer that she has resented yet needed, kills herself.

In *Faith Healer,* Friel is saying, in a postmodern way, that there are several narratives possible in his story and that he will not control and force upon the audience one ex cathedra "reading" of the drama's events. It is as if he, although the writer, denies authority to himself and is merely one of the infinite number of possible commentators or even "crafters" of the story.

Translations (1980)

Considered Friel's masterpiece and one of the most important Irish political plays ever written, *Translations* addresses the ultimate colonization of Ireland in the early nineteenth century, brought about when the British Army Engineering Corps mapped and renamed the countryside in order to facilitate military movement and control. The mapmakers and surveyors may have been well meaning, but they participated in the devastation of an ancient culture and its replacement by the colonial culture. In the play, English is at war with Irish Gaelic, and it is winning. The struggle is symbolized microcosmically by its effect on a single family in the small town once named "Baile Beag" but is now given the colonial appellation "Ballybeg."

Translations is also about the difficulties and the failures of translating—not only between languages, but more significantly between cultures. The struggle between languages, the chief conveyors of culture, is always a struggle for power.

The play is set in a hedge school, an outlawed type of school that taught Greek and Latin through the illegal language, Irish. All such schools were eventually superseded by the national schools set up in 1831 with instruction in English. The schoolmaster is Hugh, a heavy-drinking pedagogue in his sixties who stands for the fading authority of the Celtic past. He is the father of two sons: Manus, the older, is a teacher like his father; Owen, the younger, has returned to Baile Beag from Dublin with the British Army Engineering Corps to serve as a translator and thus to aid the officers in mapping and renaming the North. Owen has integrated into the greater world of the British Empire uneasily, for he still retains feelings for his Irish culture and community.

Owen's friend, the sensitive English lieutenant Yolland, falls in love with Maire, an Irish girl, and she with him. They cannot communicate with language, but love has a powerful language of its own. The audience is led to hope, in vain, that their love and his idealizing of the beauty of the landscape and the warmth of the Irish way of life will serve as the first cable in a great bridge linking the two cultures. But *Translations* is a tragedy, and, as in history, the bridge is never to be completed, for Maire has a jealous Irish suitor, and Irish toughs don't like seeing an Englishman with an Irish woman, so one day Yolland disappears.

Assuming that his lieutenant has been captured by the Irish, Captain Lancy, the British commanding officer, orders that if Yolland is not returned, in reprisal the Baile Beag livestock will be killed, its houses torn down, and its people driven from the area. Manus, sensing a tragedy unfolding, has meanwhile left Baile Beag, but he presumably will be hunted down as a suspect in the disappearance. It is also presumed that Yolland has been murdered. Owen, the mediator, the translator, the bestrider of cultures, has failed and does not know what to do with his life now.

In the end, language, human understanding, love, and compassion have broken down and failed tragically. The play *Translations,* however, succeeds brilliantly because it clearly proves the efficacy of art in informing, delineating, circumscribing, and clarifying the seemingly insoluble problems of the postcolonial world. It deeply moves the audience to embrace in their hearts the truth that all political disasters in the end are parsed into individual human pain and suffering.

Dancing at Lughnasa (1990)
Brian Friel owes a debt to Tennessee Williams's *The Glass Menagerie* for *Dancing at Lughnasa,* his exquisitely lyrical and sentimental memory play presented through the eyes of a mature narrator who sees himself as a youth and recalls key incidents in his early family life. In the case of *Dancing at Lughnasa,* the narrator, Michael Mundy, is remembering a Ballybeg childhood; unlike Tom in *The Glass Menagerie,* he breaks through the fourth wall of the play to provide dialogue for his young persona directly. This is a daring piece of stagecraft somewhat related to Friel's double character of Gar in *Philadelphia, Here I Come!*

Lughnasa is the ancient Celtic festival honoring Lug, the god of the harvest. The events of this mood play take place during the festival time in a year in the early 1930s, but they have little to do directly with the festival except in the strikingly effective and moving scene in which the unmarried Mundy sisters—Michael's mother and four aunts—like ancient celebrants break out in a spontaneous wild and joyous dance to the music from their battery-powered radio (their cottage has not been electrified as yet).

The dance and pagan leitmotivs continue through two additional characters, the adult men within the story. Michael's father, who charms with his skillful ballroom dances, comes to visit Christine, the mother of his child and the youngest of the sisters. She hopes for marriage, and Michael longs to have a permanent father in his life within the female tribe, but it is a longing not to be fulfilled, for the father, Gerry, is just passing through.

The other male dancer is Father Jack, older brother of the Mundy sisters (and thus Michael's uncle), once a priest in Africa but now apparently in forced retirement for having "gone native" and participated in pagan rituals. He treats his surprised and apprehensive sisters to his version of a tribal dance that he witnessed. Jack was deeply moved by the "Lughnasa" in his African parish.

The audience learns that the sisters' future lives, as the adult Michael recollects them, are without much happiness or prosperity. The one professionally employed sister, Kate, a teacher in a parish school, loses her job because the community is intolerant of her brother's strange behavior and disturbing paganism. None will marry. No other child will come from the family of the disgraced priest and his sisters. But this future is now all in the past, and the mature narrator, unlike Williams's Tom, wants us to share his love of the women of his childhood, his appreciation of their strength and warmth, his pleasure in nostalgia, and his bemused affection for the weak, inadequate men he knew in his youth.

As elsewhere in Friel's dramatic canon, *Dancing at Lughnasa* is slightly marred by excessive narration. In Friel's work, the play sometimes seems more like a narrated short story than a drama with action and characterization. Yet this play is in a sense a dance of exquisite phrases as well as physical movements.

Dancing at Lughnasa continues to charm, delight, and move audiences all over the world, succeeding wonderfully because of Friel's ability to stoke the memory dramas deep within us all and to project on the stage his engagement with and yearning for the earlier, simpler times in the region of his birth. He invites us to share his passionate love of people—not as vast humanity, but as the individual, ordinary, unsung women, men, and children who comprise the people of his nation. The overriding accomplishment in *Dancing at Lughnasa* is that in it Friel the playwright aspires to—and achieves—poetry *of* the theater as well as poetry *in* the theater.

Additional Reading

Andrews, Elmer. *The Art of Brian Friel*. London: Macmillan, 1995; New York: St. Martin's Press, 1995.

Boltwood, Scott. *Brian Friel, Ireland, and the North*. Cambridge, U.K.: Cambridge Univ. Press, 2008.

Corbett, Toby. *Brian Friel: Decoding the Language of Tribe*. Dublin: Liffey Press, 2002.

Dantanus, Ulf. *Brian Friel: A Study*. London: Faber, 1988.

Friel, Brian. *Selected Plays of Brian Friel*. London: Faber and Faber, 1982; Washington, D.C.: Catholic Univ. Press of America, 1986.

Maxwell, Desmond E. S. *Brian Friel*. Lewisburg, Pa.: Bucknell Univ. Press, 1973.

O'Brien, George. *Brian Friel*. Boston: Twayne, 1989; Dublin: Gill and Macmillan, 1989.

Pine, Richard. *Brian Friel and Ireland's Drama*. New York and London: Routledge, 1990.

Roche, Anthony. *Cambridge Companion to Brian Friel*. Cambridge, U.K.: Cambridge Univ. Press, 2006.

OTHER MAJOR MODERN DRAMATISTS

HUGH LEONARD (1926–2009)

Born John Joseph Byrne in Dalkey, County Dublin, to a mother who gave him up for adoption by the Keys family, this writer first used the name "John Keyes Byrne" (he never explained why he added the extra letter to Keyes), then later took the name "Hugh Leonard" from a character in an early, unproduced play. After finishing high school, he worked for fourteen years as a civil servant in Ireland and then as a writer on both shores of the Irish Sea.

Hugh Leonard was a very witty writer with a superb style and the ability to write drama that was always finely crafted. The best known of his almost thirty plays are *Stephen D* (1962), an engrossing version of Joyce's *Portrait of the Artist as a Young Man*, and the autobiographical *Da* (1973), a perennial favorite, in which Leonard compassionately memorializes his deceased adoptive father. In *Da*, Leonard has two actors share a character as Friel did in *Philadelphia, Here I Come!* (1964).

Leonard wrote several other well-known plays. *The Au Pair Man* (1968) is an allegory concerning relations between Britain and Ireland. *Summer* (1974) presents a picnic as background to revealing how the lives of three middle-aged couples have changed over the years. *A Life* (1979) is the story of a misanthropic, self-absorbed clerk whose lies hurt family members. *Love in the Title* (1999) portrays the lives of three extraordinary women in three different decades.

Additional Reading

Leonard, Hugh. *Love in the Title*. In *New Plays from the Abbey Theatre: 1999–2001*, vol. 3, edited by Judy Friel and Sanford Sternlicht. Syracuse, N.Y.: Syracuse Univ. Press, 2003.

———. *Selected Plays of Hugh Leonard*. Gerrards Cross, U.K.: Colin Smyth, 1992; and Washington, D.C.: Catholic Univ. of America Press, 1992.

———. *Stephen D*. London: Evans, 1962.

JOHN B. KEANE (1928–2002)

An especially popular dramatist and a novelist was Kerry-born John B. Keane, whose twenty plays often rely on melodrama and sentimentality. He is best represented by the frequently revived *The Field* (1965), which is neither melodramatic nor sentimental. In this drama, a bullying patriarchal farmer takes his love for a piece of land to such an extreme that he will murder for it, and his close-knit and fearful community is willing to cover up for him. The film version, although considerably changed from the stage version, was an art house success in America.

A very enjoyable play about priests and their housekeepers, *Moll* (1971) is a sentimental comedy typical of Keane. Frequently performed by community theaters, it is occasionally revived by professional theaters. Also occasionally revived are *Big Maggie* (1969, revised 1988), about a very strong Irish mother, and *The Chastitute* (1980), in which a celibate bachelor Irish farmer tries to find a wife.

Additional Reading

Kealy, Marie Hubert. *Kerry Playwright: Sense of Place in the Plays of John B. Keane.* Selingsgrove, Pa.: Susquehanna Univ. Press, 1993.

Keane, John B. *The Field.* Cork, Ireland: Mercier, 1967.

———. *Moll.* Cork, Ireland: Mercier, 1971.

Smith, Gus, and Des Hickey. *John B.: The Real Keane.* Cork, Ireland: Mercier, 1992.

EUGENE McCABE (B. 1930)

Born in Glasgow and a graduate of University College, Cork, Eugene McCabe has devoted his dramaturgic skills and energies primarily to television, but at the 1964 Dublin Theatre Festival his *King of the Castle,* a powerful, direct, social drama, was a major success. In *King of the Castle,* McCabe, like other writers of his generation, takes on as his subject the rapacious values and shameless upward mobility of the nouveaux riches.

Barney Scober, "the king," is a vain, heartless glutton for land. His "castle" is a Big House previously owned by the local gentry. But although they possess the surroundings of the gentry, neither Scober nor his wife, Treasy, will ever have the good taste of the house's previous inhabitants. Childless, desiring an heir, and taunted for his inability to father one, Barney chooses a surrogate father, a farmhand named Lynch, to stud for his wife, and a domestic tragedy ensues.

McCabe's biographical study *Swift* (1969), directed at the Abbey by Tyrone Guthrie, was another success. Also notable are *Pull Down a Horseman* (1966) and *Gale Day* (1979).

Additional Reading

McCabe, Eugene. *King of the Castle*. Dublin: Gallery Books, 1978.
———. *Pull Down a Horseman/Gale Day*. Chester Springs, Pa.: Dufour, 1999.

TOM MAC INTYRE (B. 1931)

In style, subject, and use of poetic language, Tom Mac Intyre followed in the footsteps of Synge and Beckett. Mac Intyre was born in County Cavan to parents who were teachers. He studied English literature at University College, Dublin. His reputation was established with *Eye Winker, Tom Tinker* (1972), an episodic play about the failure of violence and the messy complications of politics within a revolutionary group. Mac Intyre's greatest theatrical success was his adaptation for the stage in 1983 (revised 1986) of Patrick Kavanagh's bitter epic poem *The Great Hunger* (1942), directed by Patrick Mason.

The Bearded Lady (1984) places the rational and the mad at odds. *Rise Up Lovely Sweeney* (1985) shows Mac Intyre's ability to blend poetic language and myth to great advantage. *Dance for Your Daddy* (1987) is Mac Intyre at his creative extremity, combining Freudianism and surrealism.

Sheep's Milk on the Boil (1994) is a contemporary folk play of great poetic vitality and innovative staging. On an island off Ireland's west coast, an earthy couple, Biddy and Matt, celebrate life as they fight with the Wrack inspector.

The experimental historical drama *Good Evening Mr. Collins* (1995) had Mac Intyre breaking new ground again as he anatomized the Irish puritanism that is anathema to this playwright of sexual joy and love for life.

Other notable plays by Mac Intyre include *Snow White* (1988), *Kitty O'Shea* (1992), *Chickadee* (1993), *The Chirpaun* (1997), *The Gallant John-Joe* (2001), and *What Happened Bridgie Cleary?* (2005), a play about a woman burned to death by her husband because he thinks she is a witch. Mac Intyre is also a poet, a short-story writer, and a novelist of distinction. He continues to reside in County Cavan.

Additional Reading

Mac Intyre, Tom. *The Great Hunger/Gallant John-Joe*. Dublin: Lilliput Press, 2002.

———. *Sheep's Milk on the Boil*. In *New Plays from the Theatre: 1993–1995*, vol. 1, edited by Christopher Fitz-Simon and Sanford Sternlicht. Syracuse, N.Y.: Syracuse Univ. Press, 1996.

THOMAS KILROY (B. 1934)

The son of a policeman, Thomas Kilroy was born in Callan, County Killkenny, and educated at University College, Dublin. Kilroy, a novelist and a university lecturer as well as a playwright, demands much ratiocination from the theater audience. He has been uniquely successful in pursuing parallel careers as a playwright of distinction and an academic critic.

Kilroy's two best-known plays are *The Death and Resurrection of Mr. Roche* (1969), a study of a middle-aged Dublin bachelor, and *Talbot's Box* (1979), the surrealistic and macabre story of a Dublin carpenter, a religious mystic who is to be canonized into "the workers' saint" by unprincipled, manipulative people. Both plays present a view of Dublin working-class and lower-middle-class life. They show it to be (at least at the time of the writing) inhabited by people afraid of the system, lacking confidence in society and themselves, sexually repressed, solipsistic and arbitrary in their values, and very solitary.

The O'Neill (1969), a historical drama set in the sixteenth century, uses the Irish military hero Hugh O'Neill and his struggle with the English as a symbol for the continuing disunity in Ireland. As the earl of Tyrone, O'Neill had been brought up in the English court and thus was in himself a site of conflict.

Tea and Sex and Sympathy (1976) is Kilroy's experiment in the theater of the absurd. The play depicts a writer's neurotic struggles with his marriage, guilt, sexual impotence, diminishing sense of identity, and—worst of all—writer's block.

Other plays by Kilroy include *Double Cross* (1986), a play about role playing on the stage and in life, and *Madam MacAdam's Traveling Theatre* (1991), in which theater and transvestitism are seen as ways of both establishing and obfuscating the chimera called identity. *The Secret Fall of Constance Wilde* (1997), a provocative play about Oscar Wilde's wife, was produced by the Abbey for the 1997 Dublin Theatre Festival and was warmly received by festival audiences, who are always interested in Oscar Wilde's family. *The Shape of Metal* (2003) is a mother-daughter play about an octogenarian female sculptor and her child who must share a dark family secret at the end of the sculptor's life.

Additional Reading

Kilroy, Thomas. *The Death and Resurrection of Mr. Roche*. London: Faber, 1969.
———. *Double Cross*. Dublin: Gallery Press, 1994.
———. *The Secret Fall of Constance Wilde*. In *New Plays from the Abbey Theatre 1996–1998*, vol. 2, edited by Judy Friel and Sanford Sternlicht. Syracuse, N.Y.: Syracuse Univ. Press, 2001.

————. *The Shape of Metal*. Dublin: Gallery Press, 2003.

————. *Talbot's Box*. Dublin: Gallery Press, 1979.

TOM MURPHY (B. 1935)

A native of Tuam in County Galway, Tom Murphy has made his reputation in Britain but has also been associated with the Abbey Theatre
in Dublin and the Druid Theatre in Galway. Murphy is a master of
characterization, and although his characters are often drawn from the
less than articulate, his dialogue is charged with an energy reminiscent of the shards of language in Harold Pinter and David Mamet.

Murphy's shocking, naturalistic tragedy *A Whistle in the Dark*
(1961) remains the high-water mark of his long career as a playwright.
Set in the English industrial town of Coventry, the play is the story
of Michael Carney, an immigrant to England and a decent, hard-
working man who, out of family loyalty, welcomes his Irish father and
brothers, "the fighting Carneys," to England. They are a corrupt and
brutal band who immediately try to take over the Coventry underworld as they did in their hometown in Ireland. Beneath their violence
and aggression are their feelings of social and ethnic inferiority.

Michael holds back at first, but in the end he accepts his father
and brothers' primitive values as the monstrous patriarch of the
tribe, Dada, goads him into fighting his youngest brother, whom
he kills in the brawl. The conflict of the play is ultimately a man's
interior struggle between conscience and tribe.

The Sanctuary Lamp (1975) is set in an abandoned church,
where from dawn to after midnight two men, former circus workers, relive their past, desecrate the church, mock the clergy, and in
the ruined sanctuary struggle like Beckett's Vladimir and Estragon
to endure limbo. *The Sanctuary Lamp* is a dark passion play, like
Christopher Fry's *A Sleep of Prisoners* (1952), which is also set in a
ruined church. *The Sanctuary Lamp* is more religiously allegorical
than it initially appears to be.

The Blue Macushla (1979), a well-crafted, suspenseful gangster thriller, depicts the Irish underworld as a reflection of New York or Chicago, while hinting at an unsuccessful attempt by certain English criminal or government agents to undermine the young nation.

The Gigli Concert (1983) shows the influence of the Hollywood gangster film of the 1930s and 1940s on Murphy. The play is both a version of and an homage to detective film noir with all the conventions of the genre, including the James Cagney–like Irish gunman. *Conversations on a Homecoming* (1985) comically depicts an emigrant's return to Ireland from America for a reunion with his drinking buddies of old. *Bailegangaire* (1985) (the title means "Town Without Laughter") is a narrative about an old woman trying to finish a story she has been telling her whole life but never being given the chance to end it.

Murphy's more recent plays include *Too Late for Logic* (1989; first version titled *The White House,* 1972), a drama about an academic who has sacrificed much to rise in his profession, only to find his career near to crashing, and *The Alice Trilogy* (2005), in which Alice, in her attic, relives three periods of her life.

Murphy's work is always profound even as he savages institutions and satirizes film and stage genres. More than many other Irish playwrights, Murphy seems to write almost entirely for the Irish audience; his playing field is the contemporary Irish psyche, with all its contradictions and all the confounding, confusing influences that fight to dominate it.

Additional Reading

Elsom, John. "Thomas Murphy." In *Contemporary Dramatists,* edited by James Vinson. London: St. James Press, 1973; New York: St. Martin's Press, 1973.

Murphy, Tom. *Bailegangaire.* London: Methuen, 2001.

———. *The Gigli Concert.* London: Methuen, 2006.

———. *Murphy Plays 5*. London: Methuen, 2006.

———. *A Whistle in the Dark*. New York: French, 1971.

Murray, Christopher, ed. Special issue on Tom Murphy. *Irish University Review* 17, no. 1 (spring 1987).

O'Toole, Fintan. *The Politics of Magic: The Work and Times of Tom Murphy*. Dublin: Raven Arts Press, 1987.

STEWART PARKER (1941–1988)

Born in East Belfast and educated at Queen's University, Belfast, Stewart Parker died of cancer before he had the opportunity to fulfill his great promise as a dramatist. He completed ten plays, however. His three historical dramas that he called a "triptych" are concerned primarily with Northern Ireland. The first is *Northern Star* (1984), in which a rebel hero of the failed 1798 rebellion recalls how the idealism of his youth led to despair. Next came *Heavenly Bodies* (1986), which discusses a playwright's responsibility to his country and his people. The best of the three is *Pentecost* (1987), which was a Field Day Theatre Company triumph. It is the story of a house in Belfast once inhabited by a bigoted Protestant woman, whose ghost regularly appears and continues to spew her hatred because the house is currently a refuge for a small group of acquaintances, both Protestant and Catholic, who are avoiding the violence accompanying the 1974 Ulster Workers General Strike, a successful unionist attempt to prevent power sharing in the province.

Parker, a philosophical writer, set for the Irish artist the task of finding or creating "a working model of wholeness" for all the people of Ireland. He believed the politicians could never do it.

Additional Reading

Parker, Stewart. *Three Plays for Ireland: Northern Star, Heavenly Bodies, Pentecost*. London: Oberon Books, 1994.

CHRISTINA REID (B. 1942)

Belfast-born and from a working-class Protestant family, Christina Reid grew up in that city of spiritual and political contestation. Like Stewart Parker's *Pentecost* and Anne Devlin's *Ourselves Alone,* Reid's most successful and most political play, *Tea in a China Cup* (1982), deals with the continuing Troubles in the North. The play was runner-up to Mary Halpin's *Semi-private,* in the one-time 1982 *Irish Times* competition for women playwrights offered in conjunction with the Dublin Theatre Festival and entered by 188 women writers. Reid, the author of ten plays, is the best-known and most professionally active playwright to come out of that competition.

Tea in a China Cup is a memory play in which members of a Protestant Belfast family relive their lives during the period between the world wars. Through the continuing tea-drinking ritual, the narrator, Beth, born about the time of World War I, sharply illuminates a woman's antiwar and antiviolence perspective on the values and the limitations of the Ulster Loyalist community into the time of the more recent Troubles. Men die, often violently, but women wait and watch and live on as if their generations and stories are all one.

Joyriders (1986) uses Sean O'Casey's *The Shadow of a Gunman* (1922) as model and prologue for an essay on the dilemma of the North. *The Belle of Belfast City* (1989) shows how three generations of a Northern Irish family are caught between political rivalries.

Additional Reading

Reid, Christina. *Christina Reid Plays 1.* London: Methuen, 1987.

NEIL DONNELLY (B. 1946)

Born in Tullamore, County Offaly, Neil Donnelly is a playwright whose work has won success in Ireland, Scotland (at the Edinburgh

Festival), England, New York, and Australia. His early plays include *Dust* (1972); *The Station Master* (1974); *Upstarts* (1980), his first Abbey play; *The Silver Dollar Boys* (1981); *Flying Home* (1983); *Chalk Farm Blues* (1984); *The Boys of Summer* (1985); *Blindfold* (1986); *Good-bye Carraroe* (1989); *The Reel McCoy* (1989); *Fire* (1995); and *The Butterfly* (1995).

The Duty Master (1995) is set at a boys' public school in England, where Irish-born Patrick O'Rourke is an English master. His wife, Sarah, is a successful artist about to enjoy a one-person exhibit that will move her into the mainstream of the British art world. But the couple is unhappy, and each is having an affair. Patrick is about to offer a divorce to Sarah so that he can marry the school secretary.

Patrick is ashamed of his rural Irish heritage. One day his brother, Michael, who has stayed on the farm with their parents in Ireland, appears without warning with a girlfriend in tow who is twenty years his junior. The conflicts of the play center on the marriage on the rocks and the Cain versus Abel theme, the perennial Irish antagonism between the son who emigrated and the son who remained at home on the land. *The Duty Master* is a well-made, pertinent, and engrossing play.

Generally speaking, Donnelly writes about those Irish who for economic reasons are facing or are living in exile in Britain or elsewhere. His characters journey through bleak landscapes: Irish ghettos in foreign cities, housing cooperatives, alien schools, and other institutions. They seem to be seeking a lost place in the universe.

Additional Reading

Donnelly, Neil. *The Duty Master*. In *New Plays from the Abbey Theatre 1993–1995*, vol. 1, edited by Christopher Fitz-Simon and Sanford Sternlicht. Syracuse, N.Y.: Syracuse Univ. Press, 1996.

———. *The Station Master*. Dublin: Co-op Books, 1982.

———. *Upstarts*. Dublin: Co-op Books, 1980.

BILLY ROCHE (B. 1949)

Billy Roche, playwright, screenwriter, and novelist, was born in Wexford, County Wexford, and continues to live there. He started entertaining as a singer and led his own musical group: the Roach Band. He turned to playwriting in the 1980s.

A prolific dramatist, Roche is best known for *The Wexford Trilogy*. In the first play, *A Handful of Stars* (1988), the setting is a pool hall where wasted hours lead a young man to break with his girlfriend and turn violent. The second play, *Poor Beasts in the Rain* (1989), takes place in a betting shop and shows an Irish family falling apart because of missed opportunities and thwarted desires. Last, *Belfry* (1991), set in a church vestry and belfry, is a romantic comedy about a meek, bell-ringing sacristan who falls in love with a married woman.

Other major plays include *Haberdashery* (1988), which depicts depressed lives in southern Ireland; *The Cavalcaders* (1993), a study of small-town workers who are singers at night; *Amphibians* (1992), concerning a father and son, Wexford fishermen, and a rite of passage; *On Such as We* (2001), which is set in a barbershop that serves as a refuge for lonely hearts, whose pains are assuaged by the owner; and *Lay Me Down Softly* (2008), which depicts the burlesque world of an old-time Irish carnival.

Additional Reading

Roche, Billy. *The Wexford Trilogy*. London: Hern, 1992.

ANNE DEVLIN (B. 1951)

An Ulster-born writer, Anne Devlin has had an Irish and a British career. Besides writing plays, she also has published short stories, written for the screen, and taught creative writing at Birmingham University. She is currently based in Belfast.

In her most significant play, *Ourselves Alone* (1985), Devlin interjects three women into nationalist history and dialogue as they struggle to survive the nationalist/Unionist violence in the 1970s. The title is a translation of one of the most inflammatory and controversial names in modern Irish history: "Sinn Fein," the political party of uncompromising nationalism that since 1922 has called for the reunification of Ireland under the republic.

In *Ourselves Alone,* however, the phrase is used ironically because it refers to the women who alone resist the propaganda and the entire lexicon of violence. The women possess their own bodies, which slogan-chanting men desire, but the women will not allow their bodies to be politically so inscribed. The mocking, antinationalist, revisionist spirit of Sean O'Casey informs this powerful play.

Did You Hear the One about the Irishman? (1981), reminiscent of *Romeo and Juliet* or *West Side Story,* is about a Protestant girl and a Catholic boy in love who continue seeing each other even after terrorist paramilitias warn them to end the relationship. When they refuse, they are murdered. Sectarian hate is presented as overriding all human values. *After Easter* (1994), in which the antagonists fighting over a woman's soul are a Communist father and a Catholic mother, is more of a feminist drama than a political play.

Additional Reading

Devlin, Anne. *After Easter.* London: Faber, 1994.
———. *Joyriders and Did You Hear the One about the Irishman?* London: Heinneman, 1993.
———. *Ourselves Alone.* London: Faber, 1986.

MARIE JONES (B. 1951)

(Sarah) Marie Jones, a fine actress as well as a fine playwright, was born in East Belfast within sight of the Harland and Wolff Shipyard. She remains based in Belfast. Her twenty-five plays have had successful productions in Dublin, London, and New York, and her forte is comedy that straddles and crosses the Ulster border.

Jones's first play was *The Hamster Wheel* (1990). *A Night in November* (1995) is a brilliant one-man show in which a Protestant Ulsterman, a clerk who is barely satisfied with his life, has attended the Northern Ireland versus Republic of Ireland World Cup soccer qualifying match in Windsor Park Stadium, Belfast, and is disgusted by the anti-Catholic bigotry at a game he loves. "Disguised" as a Catholic, he sneaks off to Dublin and flies to New York with a planeload of fans to support Ireland in the 1994 World Cup. Welcomed and embraced there, he learns that the people of Ireland, regardless of their religion, share a common humanity and patriotism.

In *Women on the Verge of HRT* (1996), Anna and Vera, two friends, travel from Belfast to Donegal for the popular singer Daniel O'Donnell's annual At Home Concert. They are coming closer to the time in their lives in which they might need hormone replacement therapy; that is, they are in their forties. Daniel is a lifeline in their otherwise drab and disappointing lives. One is divorced and angry because her former husband has married a younger woman and had another child, and the other is unsatisfied in her marriage. They share a hotel room, flirt with a waiter who looks like O'Donnell, and after a few drinks fantasize about their lives and their desires. The play sparkles with sardonic wit as Anna and Vera whip out one-liners that rip into men and marriage.

Stones in His Pockets (1996) is Jones's most successful play. In it, a Hollywood production company comes to County Kerry to shoot a romantic epic set early in the twentieth century. A tragedy strikes, and the American bosses make things worse through their arrogance and insensitivity.

Additional Reading

Jones, Marie. *A Night in November.* Dublin: New Island Books, 1995; London: Nick Hern Books, 1996.

———. *Stones in His Pockets.* London: Nick Hern, 2000.

———. *Women on the Verge of HRT.* London: Samuel French, 1998.

FRANK McGUINNESS (B. 1953)

Like Brian Friel a son of the North, Frank McGuinness was born in Buncrana, County Donegal. He graduated from University College, Dublin, and began his writing career with poetry. McGuinness is currently one of several internationally recognized Irish dramatists. His first play was *Factory Girls* (1982), in which a factory and its female employees fight to survive in competition with cheap foreign labor. *The Bird Sanctuary* (1984), set in a house in a Dublin suburb overlooking a bird sanctuary, followed. *Baglady* (1985) is a moving monologue of life on the streets.

But it was McGuinness's devastatingly powerful and insightful examination of the roots and degree of Unionist Northern Ireland's intransigence, *Observe the Sons of Ulster Marching Towards the Somme* (1985), that electrified audiences in Ireland, Britain, and the United States when it was first produced. It still does in revivals.

Observe the Sons of Ulster Marching Towards the Somme is the story of eight men of the famous and doomed Thirty-sixth Ulster Division of the British army in France in World War I, which courageously went over the top and walked to destruction on 1 July 1916 in the military debacle called the battle of the Somme. The play begins in the present—in the mind of Pyper, the one survivor of a squad of eight, as he is dying of old age in a hospital. Written in four sections, it relives within his mind and with aid of ghosts the dynamics of the relationships that both torment and weld together the squad.

The men, including young Pyper, come from different walks of Ulster life, and they pair off according to class, politics, and sexual orientation as they train and prepare themselves for battle. Finally, they go into the holocaust as a unit of committed Orangemen who are, in a perhaps convoluted way, fighting for possession of Ulster by sacrificing themselves in France.

In *Mary and Lizzie* (1989), Irish women employees in nineteenth-century London interpret Marx and Engels. *The Bread Man* (1990) is the story of a middle-aged man who loses touch with reality while dealing with the death of his father. It is poetic but lacking in specificity.

The frequently produced and ever so topical *Someone Who'll Watch over Me* (1992) was another international success. It is a play about three men—an Irishman, an American, and an Englishman—seized by Arab kidnappers in Beirut and held hostage. They struggle to maintain their sanity and humanity in the face of appalling living conditions and despair. Ultimately, though, the play is as much about resolving Irish-English mutual prejudices and stereotypes as it is about the cruelty of the random, unjust imprisonment of hostages.

Other plays by Frank McGuinness include *Carthaginians* (1988), a play about the impact of Bloody Sunday on the people of Derry; *Innocence* (1996), which portrays the life of the artist Caravaggio; *Mutabilities* (1997), which deals with the seventeenth-century London Gunpowder Plot; *The Storm* (1998), which depicts mid-nineteenth-century Russia at its worst; and *Dolly West's Kitchen* (1999), a World War II play set in Donegal, where the borders crossed are not only international, but also moral, marital, and sexual.

Barbaric Comedies (2000) presents a tragicomedy about greed and passion. *The Gates of Gold* (2002) is about gender confusion, the theater couple Hilton Edwards and Micheál MacLiammóir, and the founding of the Dublin Gate Theatre. *Speaking Like Magpies* (2005) deals with a contest of female wills. *There Came a Gypsy Riding* (2007) is set in the West of Ireland, where a family secret will be exposed, and *The Tragedy from the Sea* (2008) has a woman trapped in an unhappy marriage and longing for the sea.

Additional Reading

Jordon, Eamonn. *The Feast of Famine: The Plays of Frank McGuinness.* Bern: Peter Lang, 1997.

Lojek, Helen. *Contexts for Frank McGuinness's Drama.* Washington, D.C.: Catholic Univ. of America Press, 2004.

———. *The Theatre of Frank McGuinness: Stages of Mutability.* Dublin: Carysfort Press, 2002.

McGuinness, Frank. *Dolly West's Kitchen.* In *New Plays from the Abbey Theatre 1999–2001,* vol. 3, edited by Judith Friel and Sanford Sternlicht. Syracuse, N.Y.: Syracuse Univ. Press, 2003.

———. *Observe the Sons of Ulster Marching Towards the Somme.* London: Faber, 1986.

———. *Someone Who'll Watch over Me.* London: Faber: 1992.

Mikahi, Hiroko. *Frank McGuinness and His Theatre of Paradox.* Gerrards Cross, U.K.: Colin Smythe, 2002.

MICHAEL HARDING (B. 1953)

Born in County Cavan and residing there today, Michael P. Harding is a novelist as well as a dramatist. Six of Harding's plays have been produced at the Abbey, commencing with *Strawboys* (1988) and including *Una Pooka* (1990), *The Misogynist* (1992), *Hubert Murray's Widow* (1996), *Sour Grapes* (1997), and *Amazing Grace* (1998).

Hubert Murray's Widow is a shockingly powerful play about the continuing border war between the IRA and the Royal Ulster Constabulary. It combines sexual passion and betrayal with the revenge of a ghost. The surprise ending is riveting.

Sour Grapes expresses Harding's anger and disillusion with the Catholic hierarchy and priesthood as well as with the contemporary Catholic Church. In this play, a new bishop who has come from academic life is accused of sexually abusing one of his former seminarians, a mentally unstable young man. The investigation, handled very badly and primarily at the expense of the victim, provokes deep thought in the audience and raises the question, Who can be trusted with the souls—and, indeed, the bodies—of the young?

Amazing Grace is about the IRA and a crisis of faith in a member of the Royal Ulster Constabulary, a theme Harding shares with his contemporary dramatist Sebastian Barry. The more recent *Birdie Birdie* (2004) is a wild farce in which a lonely, bedridden woman rambles on, remembering the man who deserted her, but who turns up again after all. *The Tinker's Curse* (2007) depicts the damaging effects of the travelers' world on the lives of other people. *Is There Balm in Gilead?* (2007) is a recent Harding work.

Additional Reading

Harding, Michael. *Hubert Murray's Widow*. In *New Plays from the Abbey Theatre, 1993–1995*, vol. 1, edited by Christopher Fitz-Simon and Sanford Sternlicht. Syracuse, N.Y.: Syracuse Univ. Press, 1996.

———. *Sour Grapes*. In *New Plays from the Abbey Theatre 1996–1998*, vol. 2, edited by Judy Friel and Sanford Sternlicht. Syracuse, N.Y.: Syracuse Univ. Press, 2001.

SEBASTIAN BARRY (B. 1955)

Sebastian Barry was born in Dublin and educated at Trinity College. He later served Trinity College as a Writing Fellow in 1965–66. He is currently living with his family in County Wicklow. Barry is a novelist and a poet as well as a playwright who achieved international acclaim with productions of the heartbreaking memory play *The Steward of Christendom* (1995) in Ireland, Great Britain, the United States, Australia, and New Zealand.

The Steward of Christendom is the story of Thomas Dunne, a former superintendent of the Dublin Metropolitan Police and a haunted man who looks back on his life and work during the early years of the twentieth century when the loyalty of many Irish were divided, indeed fractured. Barry's maternal great-grandfather, once a high-ranking Dublin police officer, provided the inspiration for the play.

Barry's dramatic work is highly poetical and wide ranging in subject matter. *Boss Grady's Boys* (1988) is a pastoral play about the vulnerability of the old. *Prayers of Sherkin* (1990) is about Quaker life in Ireland's west during the late nineteenth century. *White Woman Street* (1992) has an American setting, taking place in the early years of the twentieth century and dealing with the dispossessed.

Our Lady of Sligo (1998) is the story of Mai O'Hara, once the first woman in Sligo to wear trousers but now lying in a hospital bed, dying of cancer and alcoholism as she remembers her broken marriage and problems of the Irish Catholic middle class after the Civil War ended in 1923. *Whistling Psyche* (2004) finds two people between nightfall and dawn in a cold waiting room; one is a cross-dressing doctor, and the other is Florence Nightingale. Both share a passion for reform. *The Pride of Parnell Street* (2007) has two interweaving monologues that tell the story of the marriage of petty criminals, the violence that ends it, and the husband's final act of redemption.

Additional Reading

Barry, Sebastian. *The Only True History of Lizzie Finn / The Steward of Christendom / White Woman Street: Three Plays.* London: Methuen, 1995.

———. *Our Lady of Sligo.* London: Methuen, 1998.

———. *Prayers of Sherkin / Boss Grady's Boys: Two Plays.* London: Methuen, 1990.

Mahoney, Christina Hunt, ed. *Out of History: Essays on the Writing of Sebastian Barry.* Washington, D.C.: Catholic Univ. of America Press, 2006.

NIALL WILLIAMS (B. 1958)

Born in Dublin, Niall Williams graduated from University College, Dublin, and now lives in West Clare. He is a novelist and nonfiction writer as well as a dramatist. His first play, produced at the Abbey, was *The Murphy Initiative* (1991), a play about Caherconn, a village on County Clare's Atlantic west coast.

A Little Like Paradise (1995) takes place in and around Jay Feeney's grocery and bar in Caherconn. The play focuses on the dreams, illusions, and follies of the inhabitants of this atrophying community, seemingly forgotten on the western edge of Europe. The infrastructure of the community has crumbled; most of all, it needs a hospital. The local political leader is ineffective in the Dail, although a great talker locally.

A middle-age love affair is central to the play, and an elderly alcoholic provides comic relief when he "dies" in the bar and is resurrected, becoming a religious celebrity as he recounts his life-after-death experience. The tragic figure in the play is Father McInerney, who tries to keep the community together even as he is dying of cancer and struggling with his weakening faith.

The community, Caherconn, may be doomed to extinction, but it is loved by some, and they will mourn its demise because the hometown remembered as it was or could have been seems, in recollection, "a little like paradise."

The Way You Look Tonight (1998) is set in a rural post office. It depicts the breakdown of a family for lack of communication.

Additional Reading

Williams, Niall. *A Little Like Paradise.* In *New Plays from the Abbey Theatre 1993–1995,* vol. 1, edited by Christopher Fitz-Simon and Sanford Sternlicht. Syracuse, N.Y.: Syracuse Univ. Press, 1996.

DONAL O'KELLY (B. 1958)

A talented stage and film actor, Dublin-born Donal O'Kelly is also a prolific playwright. Among O'Kelly's stage works are *Bat the Father, Rabbit the Son* (1988), in which a self-made businessman tries to understand the meaning of his life by trying to comprehend his father's experiences. *Mamie Sighs* (1990), O'Kelly's first play produced at the Abbey, presents a lonely woman's recollections of a lifetime. In *The Dogs* (1992), a family has a Christmas dinner from hell. *Hughie on the Wires* (1993) is a thriller about the power of the media to affect lives. *Trickledown Town* (1994) depicts the adventures of an Irishman who comes to represent the World Bank in Jamaica.

O'Kelly's most amazing play is *Catalpa: The Movie* (1995), a "movie-treatment version" of an epic rescue of Fenians from the penal colony in Australia in the nineteenth century. It is a one-man show in which the actor plays all twenty-six parts *and* the scenery! O'Kelly was the first to perform it, and, indeed, he may be the only human capable of so doing.

Asylum! Asylum! (1995), O'Kelly's second Abbey production, is a compassionate, polemic drama about the Irish government's indifference to asylum seekers. A family civil war takes place between a sister and a brother—the former an activist lawyer, the latter an ambitious immigration officer—as they battle over the life of a Ugandan refugee. O'Kelly is a writer and activist with a finely honed social conscience. The play is immediately relevant to events concerning the treatment of asylum seekers in Ireland and elsewhere today.

The Business of Blood (1995) is a true story about the arms industry, specifically warplane manufacturing. *Judas of the Gallarus* (1999) is about Jock, a deserter at the time of the Civil War who is waiting for a vessel to take him out of Ireland and who meets Noreem, a young schoolteacher. *The Hand* (2002) shows the hard life in Dublin in the 1920s.

Additional Reading

O'Kelly, Donal. *Asylum! Asylum!* In *New Plays from the Abbey Theatre 1993–1995*, vol. 1, edited by Christopher Fitz-Simon and Sanford Sternlicht. Syracuse, N.Y.: Syracuse Univ. Press, 1996.

———. *Catalpa: The Movie*. London: Nick Hern, 1997.
———. *Judas of the Gallarus*. London: Methuen, 1999.

DERMOT BOLGER (B. 1959)

Dermot Bolger was born in the northern Dublin suburb of Finlas. He is a prolific playwright who has also tried his hand at the novel. Bolger writes dramas featuring working-class characters who are uneasy in the changing Irish society. He also explores the question of "Irishness" in modern Ireland.

Bolger has written many plays over the years. *The Lament for Arthur Cleary* (1989) is about exhausted and debilitated Ireland in the 1980s. *Blinded by the Light* (1990) features Mormon missionaries challenged by their experiences in Ireland. *One Last White Horse* (1991) is about drugs and a lost generation of Dubliners. *April Bright* (1995) centers on the house of newlyweds that is haunted by past tragedies.

In *The Passion of Jerome* (1999), a successful businessman who has lived lies is now confronting the supernatural. *Consenting Adults* (2000) shows a couple deeply engaged in sexual adventure. In *From These Green Heights* (2005), two Dublin families are portrayed over two generations. And *Walking the Road* (2007) remembers the Irish poet Francis Ledwidge, who died fighting for Britain in World War I.

Additional Reading

Bolger, Dermot. *Dermot Bolger Plays 1*. London: Methuen, 2000.

VINCENT WOODS (B. 1960)

Born on a small farm in County Leitrim, Vincent Woods attended University College, Dublin, for a year and then spent much time in

Australia and New Zealand. Although *John Henry* and *Tom John* (1991), two short plays, constituted Woods's beginning as a playwright, his playwriting career really got started with two Druid Theatre successes: *At the Black Pig's Dyke* (1992), whose title comes from the mythological name for the border between Ulster and the rest of Ireland, and *Song of the Yellow Bittern* (1994).

At the Black Pig's Dyke, a technically innovative and poetically driven drama, is a love story. Two lovers, one Catholic and one Protestant, are seeking peace and happiness on the troubled border. Mummers in masks, who are not only entertainers but also murderers (IRA operatives in disguise), fuse the archetypal and the contemporary in a play that is both tragic and humorous.

Set in County Leitrim in the past and in the present, *Song of the Yellow Bittern* is a love story and ghost story simultaneously, based on a famous 1828 paternity suit in which a Protestant woman accused a Catholic priest of having fathered her stillborn child. Woods depicts the tragic repetition of history as the same basic set of events occurs in succeeding generations.

A Cry from Heaven (2005) is Woods's version of the legend of Deirdre and Naoise. *Winter* (2005) has a middle-aged prostitute and a middle-aged married businessman going to a hotel room, but he is unable to understand why he cannot conclude the transaction.

Additional Reading

Woods, Vincent. *The Colour of Language*. Dublin: Daedalus, 1994.

JIMMY MURPHY (B. 1962)

Born in Manchester, England, to Irish immigrant parents, Murphy was brought to Dublin's inner city at the age of six. Dublin is still Murphy's base. He worked as a laborer for years before he turned to playwriting. His major plays are *Brothers of the Brush* (1993), the story of Dublin house painters working off the books, and *The Kings of the Kilburn High Road* (2000), which depicts the sad lives and unfulfilled dreams of Irish construction workers in England.

A Picture of Paradise (1996) focuses on street life in inner-city Dublin. *The Muesli Belt* (2001) shows the ravages of gentrification on the inhabitants of inner-city Dublin, and *The Castlecomer Jukebox* (2004) is a play about an old-fashioned band on its last legs and trying to relive former glory.

Additional Reading

Murphy, Jimmy. *Brothers of the Brush*. London: Oberon, 1995.
———. *The Muesli Belt*. In *New Plays from the Abbey Theatre 1999–2001*, vol. 3, edited by Judy Friel and Sanford Sternlicht. Syracuse, N.Y.: Syracuse Univ. Press, 2003.
———. *A Picture of Paradise*. In *Dazzling Dark: New Irish Plays*, selected and introduced by Frank McGuinness. London: Faber, 1996.

DECLAN HUGHES (B. 1963)

Born in Dublin, Declan Hughes is an award-winning playwright, director, and popular novelist. His best-known plays are *Twenty Grand* (1998) and *Shiver* (2003), a satire on the new Dublin business culture and entrepreneurs who are without social values. Other plays include *Digging for Fire* (1991), *Halloween Night* (1992), and *Boomtown: A City Comedy* (1999).

Additional Reading

Hughes, Declan. *Plays I*. London: Methuen, 1998.
———. *Shiver*. London: Methuen, 2003.

10

Marina Carr and the New Voices

MARINA CARR (B. 1964)

Marina Carr is the most significant and successful female Irish playwright since Lady Gregory. Her powerfully original plays have changed the ways women have been and will be represented in Irish drama at the expense of patriarchy and nationalist fervor.

Carr was born in the Midlands' County Offaly, the daughter of the playwright and novelist Hugh Carr. Carr graduated from University College, Dublin, and has had a remarkable career, including serving as writer in residence at the Abbey Theatre and Trinity College, Dublin. She now lives in County Kerry.

Her plays, mainly tragedies of rural Irish life and based on classical Greek models, have had successful runs in Dublin at the Abbey, in London in the West End and at the Royal Court, and in New Jersey at the McCarter Theatre. They depict the struggles of Irish women who are often beset by male brutality and the tragedies of rural Irish life. Carr is a classicist who is entranced by the power of Greek mythology and who deals in black humor.

Carr's early performed dramas include *Low in the Dark* (1989), a neophyte's absurdist farce exploring the landscape of sexuality while attacking sexism in language and the imagery of religion and paying homage to Beckett. *The Deer's Surrender* (1990) is also influenced by Beckett. *This Love Thing* (1991) analyzes love through the perspective of Renaissance artists. In *Ullaloo* (1991), a man and a woman strive for identity and meaning in life and death.

The Mai (1994), a major success at the Abbey, is a tragic memory play that tells the story of four generations of women, each of whose life is a tangle of dreams, fantasies, and heart-wrenching disappointments, mitigated only by the love and sense of matriarchy the women share.

Portia Coughlin (1996) was commissioned by Ireland's National Maternity Hospital as part of its centenary celebration, and Carr based herself in the hospital while writing it. The play, like *The Mai* a woman's drama, portrays a woman in despair who is haunted by the memory of her dead twin brother, who drowned fifteen years earlier.

By the Bog of Cats (1998) is a brilliant retelling of Euripides' *Medea* in the Irish Midlands. *On Raftery's Hill* (2000) is a very dark tragedy of ugly rural life involving parental abuse, fear, and incest. Returning to classical Greek drama, Carr's *Ariel* (2002) retells Euripides' *Iphigenia at Aulis*.

Meat and Salt (2003) depicts in fairy-tale fashion a young princess banished from the kingdom by her father. *Women and Scarecrow* (2006) concerns a worn-out woman who has birthed eight children and now faces death. *The Cordelia Dream* (2008) is a two-hander in which a woman and an older man question the element of hatred in their competition in art. *Marble* (2009) focuses on two male friends who dream about each other's wives, those desperate housebound wives, and four lives unraveling.

Plays

Portia Coughlin (1996)

It is Portia's thirtieth birthday. She has been married for thirteen years to a successful businessman and has given birth to three sons, but she is unhappy and depressed, and she has little love for the institutions of marriage and motherhood because of the demands society makes of those institutions. Her escape is through affairs, but they make her even less stable as her life dissolves in fears and fantasies.

By the Bog of Cats (1998)

Hester Swayne is Carr's Medea. She is the common-law wife of a man named Carthage, and they have a daughter. Carthage has abandoned Hester to marry a wealthy farmer's daughter. It is his opportunity for upward mobility and higher status in the Midlands community. Hester still loves Carthage and is in denial that the marriage will occur. When Carthage asks her to leave their home, she will not take his abuse lying down, and, as a result, the community will suffer too. Instead of leaving, Hester in vengeance sets fire to the house and Carthage's new farm, burning everything, even the animals, to ashes. She then decides on suicide. She takes her daughter into her arms and kills her, then stabs herself to death when all have seen the havoc she has created.

Additional Reading

Carr, Marina. *By the Bog of Cats.* In *New Plays from the Abbey Theatre 1996–1998*, vol. 2, edited by Judy Friel and Sanford Sternlicht. Syracuse, N.Y.: Syracuse Univ. Press, 2001.

———. *The Cordelia Dream.* Dublin: Gallery Press, 2008.

———. *The Mai.* Dublin: Gallery Press, 1995.

———. *Plays: One.* London: Faber, 1999.

———. *Portia Coughlin.* London: Faber, 1996.

———. *Woman and Scarecrow.* London: Faber, 2006.

Leeney, Cathy, and Anna McMullan. *The Theatre of Marina Carr: Before Rules Were Made.* Dublin: Carysfort Press, 2003.

JACQUELINE McCARRICK (B. 1967)

A graduate of Middlesex University and Trinity College, Dublin, Jacqueline McCarrick is a playwright, poet, and short-story writer. She was writer-in-residence in 2007 at the Tyrone Guthrie Centre in County Monaghan. McCarrick's first produced play, *The Mush-room Pickers* (2006), premiered in London. In it, a pregnant woman employed as a mushroom picker in rural Ireland is found attractive by a dangerous and wanted IRA operative.

Leopardville (2010) is a play about the Troubles in 1990. A gang of young men rob a pub in a border town and the crime turns to horror.

The Moth-Hour has had several distinguished readers and is about to be produced. Set in County Monaghan, the play centers on a young man who is trapped as a clerk in the family grocery and whose former lover returns to town, causing old hurts to appear again.

EUGENE O'BRIEN (B. 1967)

Eugene O'Brien was born in Dublin but grew up in Edenderry, County Offaly. He is an actor who also writes for television and film. O'Brien's first play, *Scorpion* (1993), is about the contemporary Dublin scene: relationships, sex, and games. *America '87* (1995) depicts an Irishman's American bus odyssey. *Checking for Squirrels* (1995) is an Irish odyssey full of eccentrics. *Eden* (2001) is a comic two-hander about a man with two loves. The film version was produced in 2008. *Savoy* (2004), a play of revelations and regrets, is set in a provincial town in County Offaly where the Savoy cinema is closing forever and deserves a wake.

Additional Reading

O'Brien, Eugene. *Eden.* London: Methuen, 2001.
———. *Savoy.* London: Methuen, 2004.

ENDA WALSH (B. 1967)

Dublin-born but now London-based Enda Walsh attended secondary school with novelist, dramatist, and screenwriter Roddy Doyle.

Walsh first wrote plays for the Dublin Youth Theatre and then moved to Cork, where he wrote for the Graffiti Theatre Company.

In *The Ginger Ale Boy* (1995), a Cork boy who is a talented ventriloquist cannot achieve his dream. *Suckling Dublin* (1997) involves young Dubliners, alcohol, and a rape. Walsh's first hit play, *Disco Pigs* (1998), depicting two buddies with a secret language, launched an impressive playwriting career. *Misterman* (1999) depicts Inishfree's self-appointed guardian of morality judging the community. *The Small Things* (2004) tells the story of a man and a woman whose mundane conversation reveals horror and brutality. *The New Electric Ballroom* (2005) is about three sisters trapped in a remote fishing village remembering romances of long ago. In *The Walworth Farce* (2006), three Irish men in London drink and eat while five people are killed. Walsh also writes for the screen and radio.

Additional Reading

Walsh, Enda. *Disco Pigs*. London: Nick Hern, 1998.
———. *Misterman*. London: Nick Hern, 2001.
———. *The New Electric Ballroom*. London: Nick Hern, 2008.
———. *The Small Things*. London: Nick Hern, 1997.
———. *The Walworth Farce*. London: Nick Hern, 2007.

CHRISTIAN O'REILLY (B. 1968)

London born of Irish parents, Christian O'Reilly was brought at the age of eight to live in Listowel, County Kerry, where the playwright John B. Keane once owned a pub. O'Reilly received a bachelor's degree in communications studies from Dublin City University and a postgraduate degree in business from University College, Dublin. He has written several successful plays. His first full-length play is *The Good Father* (2002), about a man and a woman, strangers at a New Year's Eve party, hooking up. *The Avenue* (2005) delves into the revelations of family history in comic and moving ways. *Is This about Sex?* (2007) is a relationship comedy about gender and sex. Two couples switch partners, but no one is happy.

Additional Reading

O'Reilly, Christian. *Is This about Sex?* London: Methuen, 2009.

STELLA FEEHILY (B. 1969)

Stella Feehily is an actress as well as a playwright. Although London born, she grew up in County Donegal. *Duck* (2003), her first full-length play, has two teenage girls growing up in a corrupt city where it is very hard to be good when elders are not. *O Go My Man* (2006) (the title is an anagram for the word *monogamy*) is a sexually explicit play about the new Ireland and love struggling to survive monogamy. Her latest play, *Think Global, Fuck Local* (2008), deals with the lives of humanitarian aid workers. Feehily's plays have been enthusiastically received in Dublin, London, and New York.

Additional Reading

Feehily, Stella. *Duck*. London: Nick Hern, 2003.
———. *O Go My Man*. London: Nick Hern, 2006.

PAUL MEADE (B. 1969)

Paul Meade was born in California of Irish parents who brought him to Limerick at the age of eight. He trained at the Samuel Beckett Centre at Trinity College, Dublin, and received a master's degree in modern drama from University College, Dublin. Meade is an actor and director as well as a writer for the stage, film, and television. He is a Dublin resident.

Scenes from a Water Cooler (2001) features three male office workers and a lot of male-speak. The powerful *Skin Deep* (2003) is a contemporary revenge play full of lust, jealousy, money, death, and the body—quite worthy of the Jacobean period. *All These Guys* was first produced in 2005. In *Trousers* (2006), two middle-aged former college pals whose lives are now crumbling recall a long ago trip to New York City and the days of their youth. *Mushroom* (2007) is about Polish and Romanian immigrants in Monaghan and their problems.

EMMA DONOGHUE (B. 1969)

Born in Dublin, Emma Donoghue now resides in Canada. She is a playwright and a novelist. Her first play was *I Know My Own Heart* (1993), about an independent woman who, even in the early nineteenth century, knew what she wanted out of life. Other plays include *Ladies and Gentlemen* (1996), which deals with vaudeville stars in the late nineteenth century, and *Kissing the Witch* (1997), about women who are at the center of fantastical tales that never have a happy-ever-after ending.

Additional Reading

Donoghue, Emma. *I Know My Own Heart*. In *Six Plays by Irish Women*. Dublin: Carysfort Press, 2001.

MARK O'ROWE (B. 1970)

Born in Dublin, Mark O'Rowe has used his city background to focus on Irish urban life through powerful language, surrealism, and violence. His first play, *The Aspidistra Code* (1995), deals with a loan shark, victims, and violence. The short play *Anna's Ankle* (1997) projects a sadistic video director obsessed with a young woman's ankle. In that same year, *From Both Hips,* a comic revenge play about a man wounded by the police in a drug bust, was well received. With *Howie the Rookie* (1999), a brutal crime story, O'Rowe achieved further recognition as a playwright to be watched.

Made in China (2001) has crooks and rogue cops fighting to survive in an imaginary Dublin underworld. *The Salvage Shop* (2005) depicts the reconciliation of a dying father and his son as the son attempts to fulfill his father's lifelong dream. *Terminus* (2008) presents a serial killer who has made a pact with the devil.

O'Rowe is also a successful screenwriter.

Additional Reading

O'Rowe, Mark. *Crestfall.* London: Nick Hern, 2003.
———. *From Both Hips.* London: Nick Hern, 1999.
———. *Howie the Rookie.* London: Nick Hern, 1999.
———. *Made in China.* London: Nick Hern, 2001.
———. *Terminus.* London: Nick Hern, 2007.

RONAN NOONE (B. 1970)

Hailing from Clifden, County Connemara, Ronan Noone has made his career as an Irish playwright writing to a large extent in the United States and for American stages and audiences. His plays have Irish or American settings. He became a U.S. citizen in 2000. His most successful plays are *The Lepers of Baile Baiste* (2002), the first play in Noone's Baile trilogy, which deals with the Catholic Church abuse scandal in Ireland and how Irish society avoids responsibility; *The Gigolo of Baile Breag* (2004), a love story in which the lovers' sexual transgressions haunt them even as they bind them; and *The Blowin of Baile Gall* (2005), about an English couple in a small Irish town who experience the townspeople's narrowness, prejudice, and racial hatred.

Also admired is Noone's play *The Atheist* (2006), a one-man dark comedy about a washed-up celebrity journalist from a working-class mid-America background whose struggle for fame is self-destructive.

Additional Reading

Noone, Ronan. *The Blowin of Baile Gall.* New York: Dramatists Play Service, 2005.

MARTIN MCDONAGH (B. 1970)

Martin McDonagh was born in Camberwell, a London neighborhood, to Irish parents. His mother came from County Sligo and his father from County Galway. As a youth he spent his summers in the West of Ireland, where, like Synge, he heard and learned the Irish English spoken in the far western counties. Synge, along with Harold Pinter, Sam Shepard, and David Mamet, provided models for the language, bleak humor, brutality, menace, and pain in McDonagh's dramas.

McDonagh was discovered by the Druid Theatre in Galway, where his first play, *The Beauty Queen of Leenane* (1996), indicated that he would quickly assume a place among outstanding young Irish playwrights. This play is part of McDonagh's *Leenane Trilogy*. The second play is *A Skull in Connemara* (1997), about a man whose job is to disinter corpses so that the graves can be reused; he has to dig up his own wife, only to find her grave has been looted. And the third is *The Lonesome West* (1997), based on Sam Shepard's 1980 play *True West*; in it, two brothers whose father has just died from a shotgun accident are constantly at war with each other, and an alcoholic parish priest tries and fails to make peace between them, but then takes his own life.

The Aran Isles Trilogy followed. *The Cripple of Inishmaan* (1996) concerns an orphaned and disabled teenage boy who gets a part in the making of the famous documentary *Man of Aran* and winds up in Hollywood. *The Lieutenant of Inishmore* (2001) features a sadistic terrorist who loves to torture and bomb, but who adored his murdered cat even more. The third play in the trilogy, *The Banshees of Inisheer,* has not yet been performed or published because McDonagh says it is not yet good enough.

The Pillowman (2003), winner of awards in London and New York, is a political play reminiscent of plays by Harold Pinter and Caryl Churchill. It depicts the nightmare of a writer in a totalitarian state. *A Behanding in Seattle* (2010), a black comedy, has a criminal searching for his long-lost hand. The versatile McDonagh also wrote and directed the successful feature film *In Bruges* (2008), a macabre thriller about two Irish hit men on the loose in Belgium.

Plays

The Beauty Queen of Leenane (1996)

The Beauty Queen of Leenane is set in the kitchen–living room of a cottage in a small town in County Galway. The people seem backward in contrast to the Australian television programs they watch. The contrast is heightened by the fact that relatives return to visit from America while the men go back and forth to England to work.

This is Synge country. Maureen, a forty-year-old virgin who is at constant war with her controlling seventy-year-old mother, meets and, because of her mother's selfish interference, loses Pato, her first lover, her playboy of the Western world, who wants her to meet him in Boston so that they can continue as lovers and make a life together. The play is a black comedy with horrifying elements and sinister moments of suspense, but it also contains very witty and pointed dialogue. It is an essay on the continuing strain of violence in rural Irish culture as well as a love story with a sad ending for the heroine, as there is for Synge's Pegeen.

The Cripple of Inishmaan (1996)

Also set in the west of Ireland, this time on a remote Aran island, McDonagh's second play, *The Cripple of Inishmaan,* is about a crippled orphan boy who is ridiculed and treated roughly by the community. He feels unloved and unwanted even though he is cared for by his "aunts," two elderly sisters who are actually unrelated to him. He wants to find out how his parents died, and he longs for the love of a violent young woman ironically named Helen. When a film crew from America comes to the Aran Islands, he goes to them to see if he can get employment as an actor and is invited to Hollywood for a screen test. When he returns to Inishmaan, he finds truth and love.

The play's tone cuts back and forth cleverly from laughter to tears and is wickedly politically incorrect. McDonagh's eclectic and acerbic vision is devoted to those left behind in the development of modern, prosperous Ireland.

Additional Reading

Chambers, Lillian, and Eamonn Jordon. *The Theatre of Martin McDonagh: A World of Savage Stories.* Dublin: Caryfort Press, 2006.

McDonagh, Martin. *The Beauty Queen of Leenane and Other Plays.* New York: Vintage Books, 1996.

———. *The Cripple of Inishmaan.* New York: Vintage Books, 1998.

———. *The Lieutenant of Inishmore.* London: Methuen, 2001.

———. *The Lonesome West.* London, Methuen, 1997.

CONOR MCPHERSON (B. 1971)

Conor McPherson is one of the leading younger Irish playwrights today. The Dublin-born McPherson received his education and early indoctrination into the theater at University College, Dublin, and the school's Drama Society. His plays are produced and seen not only in Dublin now, but also in London's National Theatre and on the West End as well as on Broadway.

Although McPherson's plays are infused with mood, mystery, spirituality, religion, and deeply intriguing characterization, they are not without humor. Viewers and readers are left with the feeling that they have experienced profound poetry and are somehow different now.

McPherson's first great success was *The Weir* (1997), in which the arrival of a young woman from Dublin upsets the male patrons of a rural Irish pub, leading to revelations and confessions. The title, like the titles of other McPherson dramas, is enigmatic. A weir is a dam that holds back water—here perhaps catching fish or souls?

Dublin Carol (2000) takes place on Christmas Eve in an alcoholic undertaker's office. The lonely undertaker, estranged from his family many years ago, is eager to keep his young assistant present, only to let him go home when the whiskey is gone. His daughter appears to beg him to visit his dying wife in a hospital, which he reluctantly but mercifully agrees to do.

Shining City (2004) is set in the Dublin office of a psychiatrist who has deep secrets that must be dealt with. *The Seafarer* (2006) also takes place on Christmas Eve in the Dublin seaside suburb of Clontarf (thus the title), where a satanic figure arrives from the past (or from the sea), forcing the protagonist to play cards for his soul.

The following earlier plays served as McPherson's apprenticeship and training ground. In *Rum and Vodka* (1992), a young alcoholic relates the tale of a binge that threatens to obliterate the drab life he has been living. *The Good Thief* (1994) features a criminal on the run across Ireland from his gang bosses because he has taken with him the wife and daughter of a man they ordered him to threaten. *The Lime Tree Bower* (1995) contains three related monologues by young men whose lives are about to change for the good.

In *St. Nicholas* (1997), a jaded theater critic, in love with a young actress, meets vampires who offer him eternal life if he can fulfill their lust for blood. *Port Authority* (2001) employs interlocking monologues to explore the lives of three generations of Dublin men. *Come on Over* (2001) tells the story of a Jesuit and his childhood sweetheart as he is engaged with investigating a miracle for the Vatican.

McPherson is a prolific writer, but he is also a director who, like Martin McDonagh, also writes for film.

Additional Reading

McPherson, Conor. *Conor McPherson: Four Plays.* London: Nick Hern, 1999.
———. *McPherson: Collected Plays 2.* London: Nick Hern, 2004.
Wood, Gerald C. *Conor McPherson.* Dublin: Liffey Press, 2003.

STUART CAROLAN (B. 1971)

Dublin-based Stuart Carolan's first play, *Defender of the Faith* (2004), is set in 1986 in County Armagh when an IRA visitor arrives from Belfast looking for an informer. It is a brutally honest play about the "Troubles." *Empress of India* (2006) is a black comedy about an old and bitter Irish actor venting his misogyny. Carolan is also a journalist as well as a radio and television producer.

Additional Reading

Carolan, Stuart. *Defender of the Faith.* London: Nick Hern, 2004.

ROBERT MASSEY (B. 1975)

Playwright Robert Massey lives in Kildare. His plays have been performed in London as well as in Dublin. His background in the business world has informed his dramaturgy. *Deadline* (2006) deals with backstabbing in the business world; *Over and Out* (2008) has salesmen using skullduggery to win a significant incentive; and *Rank* (2008) is a dark comedy that finds a Dublin taxi driver turned robber in debt and deep trouble.

Additional Reading

Massey, Robert. *Rank.* London: Nick Hern, 2008.

URSULA RANI SARMA (B. 1978)

Of Irish Indian background, Sarma was brought up in County Cork. She graduated from the University of Cork in 1999. She has written nine plays, including *Touched* (1999), a story of escaping rural Irish life; *Blue* (2000), about children at the end of innocence; *Gift* (2001), in which a missionary finds horror in Ireland when he returns from Africa because of his father's death; and *Magic Tree* (2008), where love is found in a dark place.

Additional Reading

Sarma, Ursula Rani. *Touched / Blue.* London: Oberon, 2002.

GARY DUGGAN (B. 1979)

Dublin-born Garry Duggan began writing scripts at age fifteen. He studied media at the Dublin Institute of Technology. Duggan's main subject is contemporary Dublin life. His first produced play, *Monged* (2005), is a buddy play about three drugged-up Dublin men on a city odyssey. *Dedalus Lounge* (2006) is set in a grungy Dublin pub where college buddies meet to reminisce. *Trans-Euro*

Express (2008) is another buddy play, a black comedy of pals on the road on the Continent.

SEAN McLOUGHLIN (B. 1979)

Sean McLoughlin grew up in Artane, County Dublin, and began writing plays in his late twenties, most notably *Noah and the Towerflower* (2008), a comic love story about two Dubliners trying to leave their past lives behind.

IOANNA ANDERSON (B. 1979)

A Dublin resident, Ioanna Anderson was born in Edinburgh of Irish and Greek parents. She has an English degree from Trinity College, Dublin. Her first play, *Describe Joe* (2000), is a monologue spoken by a young man who has no recollection of why he has been locked out of his life. In *Words of Advice for Young People* (2004), the children of a missing writer find his remains and must bury him with dignity if they can. *Six Acts of Love* (2008) presents an elderly woman and her dysfunctional extended family's journey into rural Ireland.

Additional Reading

Anderson, Ioanna. *Six Acts of Love*. London: Nick Hern, 2008.
———. *Words of Advice for Young People*. London: Nick Hern, 2004.

LISA McGEE (B. 1981)

Derry-born Lisa McGee studied drama at Queens University, Belfast. Her *Girls and Dolls* (2006) is a Northern Ireland play about two women reliving a childhood tragedy. *Jump* (2007) is about Belfast criminals and a night of crime. *Seven Years and Seven Hours*

(2008) is a mystery play concerning a jailbird and the serial killings of schoolgirls. McGee has also written for television and is now writing for film.

Additional Reading

McGee, Lisa. *Girls and Dolls*. London: Nick Hern, 2006.

SELECTED
CRITICAL
BIBLIOGRAPHY

FILMOGRAPHY

INDEX

Selected Critical Bibliography

Bell, Sam Hanna. *The Theatre in Ulster.* Dublin: Gill and Macmillan, 1972.

Boyd, Ernest A. *The Contemporary Drama of Ireland.* Dublin: Talbot Press; London: Unwin, 1918.

———. *Ireland's Literary Renaissance.* Rev. ed. Dublin: Maunsel, 1922.

Deane, Seamus. *A Short History of Irish Literature.* London: Hutchinson, 1986.

Ellis-Furmor, Una. *The Irish Dramatic Movement.* Rev. ed. London: Methuen, 1954.

Etherton, Michael. *Contemporary Irish Dramatists.* London: Macmillan, 1989.

Fallis, Richard. *The Irish Renaissance: An Introduction to Anglo-Irish Literature.* Syracuse, N.Y.: Syracuse Univ. Press, 1977.

Fitz-Simon, Christopher. *The Irish Theatre.* London: Thames and Hudson, 1983.

Fitz-Simon, Christopher, and Sanford Sternlicht, eds. *New Plays from the Abbey Theatre 1993–1995.* Vol. 1. Syracuse, N.Y.: Syracuse Univ. Press, 1996.

Forster, R. F. *The Oxford History of Ireland.* New York: Oxford Univ. Press, 1989.

Friel, Judy, and Sanford Sternlicht, eds. *New Plays from the Abbey Theatre: 1996–1998.* Vol. 2. Syracuse, N.Y.: Syracuse Univ. Press, 2001.

———, eds. *New Plays from the Abbey Theatre: 1999–2001.* Vol. 3. Syracuse, N.Y.: Syracuse Univ. Press, 2003.

Grene, Nicholas. *The Politics of Irish Drama: Plays in Context from Boucicault to Friel.* Cambridge, U.K.: Cambridge Univ. Press, 1999.

Harris, Susan Cannon. *Gender and Modern Irish Drama.* Bloomington: Indiana Univ. Press, 2002.

Hogan, Robert Goode. *After the Irish Renaissance: A Critical History of Irish Drama since "The Plough and the Stars."* Minneapolis: Univ. of Minnesota Press, 1967; London: Macmillan, 1968.

———. *Since "Sean O'Casey" and Other Essays on Irish Drama.* Gerrards Cross, U.K.: Colin Smyth, 1983.

Hogan, Robert Goode, and Michael J. O'Neill, eds. *Joseph Holloway's Abbey Theatre: A Selection from His Unpublished Journal, Impressions of a Dublin Playgoer.* Carbondale: Southern Illinois Univ. Press, 1967.

Hunt, Hugh. *The Abbey: Ireland's National Theatre 1904–1978.* New York: Columbia Univ. Press, 1979.

Kiberd, Declan. *Inventing Ireland: The Literature of the Modern Nation.* London: Vintage, 1996.

Maxwell, D. E. S. *A Critical History of Modern Irish Drama.* Cambridge, U.K.: Cambridge Univ. Press, 1984; Washington, D.C.: Catholic Univ. of America Press, 1984.

McHugh, Roger, and Maurice Harmon. *A Short History of Anglo-Irish Literature.* Dublin: Wolfhound Press, 1982; Totowa, N.J.: Barnes and Noble, 1982.

Mercier, Vivian. *The Irish Comic Tradition.* Oxford, U.K.: Oxford Univ. Press, 1962.

Mikhail, E. H. *An Annotated Bibliography of Modern Anglo-Irish Drama.* Troy, N.Y.: Whitson, 1981.

———. *A Research Guide to Modern Irish Dramatists.* Troy, N.Y.: Whitson, 1979.

Morash, Christopher. *A History of Irish Theatre 1601–2000.* Cambridge, U.K.: Cambridge Univ. Press, 2002.

Murray, Christopher. *Twentieth-Century Irish Drama: Mirror up to Nation.* Manchester, U.K.: Manchester Univ. Press, 1997; Syracuse, N.Y.: Syracuse Univ. Press, 2000.

O'Connor, Ulick. *Celtic Dawn: A Portrait of the Irish Literary Renaissance.* London: Hamish Hamilton, 1984.

O hAodha, Micheál. *The Abbey—Then and Now.* Dublin: Abbey Theatre, 1969.

Richards, Shaun, ed. *Cambridge Companion to Twentieth-Century Irish Drama.* Cambridge, U.K.: Cambridge Univ. Press, 2003.

Robinson, Lennox. *Ireland's Abbey Theatre: A History 1899–1951.* London: Sidgwick and Jackson, 1951; Port Washington, N.Y.: Kennikat, 1968.

Roche, Anthony. *Contemporary Irish Drama: From Beckett to McGuinness.* Dublin: Gill and Macmillan, 1994.

Sihra, Melissa. *Women in Irish Drama: A Century of Authorship and Representation.* New York: Palgrave Macmillan, 2007.

Trotter, Mary. *Ireland's National Theaters: Political Performance and the Origins of the Irish Dramatic Movement.* Syracuse, N.Y.: Syracuse Univ. Press, 2001.

Waters, Maureen. *The Comic Irishman.* Albany: State Univ. of New York Press, 1984.

Watt, Stephen. *Joyce, O'Casey, and the Irish Popular Theater.* Syracuse, N.Y.: Syracuse Univ. Press, 1991.

Worth, Katherine. *The Irish Drama of Europe from Yeats to Beckett.* Atlantic Highlands, N.J.: Humanities Press, 1978.

Filmography

Synge	*Playboy of the Western World*	1962
Synge	*Playboy of the Western World*	1975 (television production)
Synge	*Playboy of the Western World*	1994 (video recording of Druid Theatre Stage Performance)
O'Casey	*Juno and the Paycock*	1930
O'Casey	*The Plow and the Stars*	1936
Beckett	*Beckett on Film*	2001 (Gate Theatre production of nineteen plays on film, VHS, and DVD)
Leonard	*Da* (Home Before Night)	1988
Keane	*The Field*	1990
Friel	*Dancing at Lughnasa*	1998
O'Brien	*Eden*	2008

Index

SANFORD STERNLICHT is emeritus professor of English at Syracuse University, where he taught Irish, American, and British drama. His Syracuse University Press books on drama include *A Reader's Guide to Modern American Drama* (2002) and *A Reader's Guide to Modern British Drama* (2004). He has also edited *The Selected Plays of Padraic Colum* (1986) and coedited *New Plays from the Abbey Theatre*, volume 1 (1996, with Christopher Fitz-Simon) and volumes 2 and 3 (2001 and 2003, with Judy Friel). In summers from 1994 through 2007, he taught the course "Irish Drama: Politics and War" for American students at Trinity College, Dublin.